❦
Tony Clark's
New Blueberry Hill
Cookbook

TONY CLARK'S
NEW BLUEBERRY HILL
COOKBOOK

COMPILED AND EDITED BY
ARLYN HERTZ

DOWN EAST BOOKS

Copyright © 1990 by Arlyn Patricia Hertz and Anthony Clark
Cover illustration © 1984 by Sabra Field
ISBN 0-89272-286-X
Library of Congress Catalog Card Number 90-61409
Designed by Faith Hague/Watermark Design
Composition by Typeworks, Belfast, Maine
Printed at Bookcrafters, Fredericksburg, Va.

5 4 3 2

Down East Books
Camden, Maine 04843

Contents

❦
INTRODUCTION

Ask any cook at Blueberry Hill what question the guests most often asked and the unanimous reply would be, *So, when is there going to be a new Blueberry Hill cookbook?*

The adjective "new" is used because the previous owner of the Inn, Elsie Masterton, wrote several cookbooks featuring recipes and menus from the very successful restaurant she ran at Blueberry Hill during the 1950s and 1960s. The best known, *The Blueberry Hill Cookbook,* was first published in 1959 and is still printed and distributed by Down East Books, of Camden, Maine.

But that was nearly thirty years ago, and things have changed.

The present owner and proprietor of the inn, Tony Clark, moved to Blueberry Hill with his then wife, Martha Tatman, in 1968. They began an era of new cuisine that combined Martha's "down-home, home-grown, country-fresh" cooking with Tony's French and English flair for elegance and detail. Thus a new style of cooking has evolved at the inn: a style that has earned the inn its reputation for fine and elegant haute cuisine; a style that reflects Tony's philosophy of food preparation and presentation.

Today, under Tony's direction, the inn continues to operate under that deliberately simple and consistent philosophy of food: to serve foods that focus on the fresh, seasonal, and, whenever possible, regional; that utilize the best ingredients available and rely on quality, not exotica; are unusual but not unrecognizable; are prepared to delight the eye as well as the palate—in short, foods that have been described as elegant, gourmet, country-simple yet sophisticated, and just plain delicious.

After years of inquiries and requests, compliments and questions, we saw a clear need for a cookbook containing recipes for many of the dishes served at Blueberry Hill from the early 1970s right up to the present. As a collection of favorite recipes, it features those most special, and many times sinfully rich, dishes served at Blueberry Hill. As guests enter the dining room after a day of vigorous skiing or hiking, or even "rigorous relaxation," they temporarily abandon calorie counting and cholesterol watching in favor of splurging on such temptations as shrimp tartlets, tomato bisque, beef tenderloin with Irish Whiskey Sauce, or lime cheesecake, not to mention those ubiquitous and decadent chocolate chip cookies.* The collection also serves as an appreciation of and tribute to all the people who have cooked at Blueberry Hill. But most important, it will give old friends and new an opportunity to retaste, or experience for the first time, the best of Blueberry Hill's cuisine.

So now, in response to that much-asked question . . . Here is *The New Blueberry Hill Cookbook*.

*Tony still refuses to reveal this recipe! The cookies are available through the Blueberry Hill mail order catalog, however.

ABOUT
BLUEBERRY HILL
OR
A HISTORY ACCORDING TO
TONY CLARK

For those of you who have visited the inn and have been subjected, perhaps more than once, to my story of Blueberry Hill, you might want to skip these next few pages and get right to the reason you bought this book—which was, I'm sure, not to listen to a long-winded Welshman reminisce, but to try for yourself some of the fine recipes included here, thus tapping into your own memories and personal history with Blueberry Hill.

But for those of you who "want to hear *his* version one more time," and for those of you new to Blueberry Hill who are interested in some background, allow me to indulge in a little history.

First of all, most people think that running a country inn is a reality born out of a long-held romantic fantasy—a vision of a way of life. I'd love to tell my story based on that notion, but it's just not the way it was.

In 1963 I was a naive nineteen-year-old Welshman with a dream of traveling the world—or at least the United States. I fantasized about life in America with no real clue as to what I would do, where I would go, or how I would survive.

In September 1964, when I landed at Logan Airport in Boston, en route to a job teaching French and coaching soccer at the Eaglebrook School in Deerfield, Massachusetts, I was still a naive young Welshman. The head of the department picked me up and I was off to experience life in America and many other firsts, all quite horrifying: madras shorts, women in curlers, big cars, and Howard Johnson's restaurants.

I settled into life at Eaglebrook and became very friendly with the art teacher, Martha, and her husband, Lou Couvert. Lou and I shared a love for nature, the mountains, and specifically, New England. That following summer Lou was killed in a tragic rock-climbing accident, and as a result I became even closer to Martha and her young son, Tim. Friendship led to romance, which led to Vermont, which led to marriage. We married in June 1968 and had a celebration at the property Martha had just bought—a place called Blueberry Hill Farm, previously owned by the Masterton family, in the remote town of Goshen, Vermont. Thus the seed was sown, but still no vision.

When Martha and I moved into the charming 1813 farmhouse situated in ideal isolation in the heart of the Green Mountain National Forest, our dream was to homestead and restore the old house. We were riding on the idealism of the late 1960s and wanted to be self-sufficient and return to nature. I had a job teaching in a private school in Burlington, and we divided our time between teaching, fixing up the house, and being a family.

However, certain changes occurred. Martha and I had a second child, our son, Christopher, and shortly thereafter the school where I taught was closed. Unemployed, I found a job in a ski shop in Rutland, and there got my first exposure to cross-country skiing. Again the seed is sown deeper, but still no vision.

Our economic situation was shaky, and we began playing with the idea of turning our farmhouse back into an inn and ski touring center. This idea, through sheer desperation, *finally* led to a vision, which led to much physical labor and renovations, which led to a reality. In December 1971 we hung out the Blueberry Hill shingle and were open for business. Hardly your romantic fantasy, as I warned earlier.

And, to our amazement and pleasure, the business grew. I was the promoter—the idea person—in charge of marketing the inn and developing the cross-country ski center. Martha focused on the inn, utilizing her artistic and aesthetic talents and her natural culinary skills, and together we began to develop Blueberry Hill as an ideal mountain retreat where one could ski and relax in the atmosphere of a restored 1813 farmhouse, and furthermore enjoy fine country cuisine, expertly and creatively prepared.

The birth of the inn and the success that followed was tremendously gratifying and rewarding, but it was also the birth of a struggle. The constant demands and pressures of innkeeping took their toll on our personal life. In 1983 Martha and I split up; I remained at Blueberry Hill and became the sole proprietor of a year-round, burgeoning business. I became more involved in the running of the kitchen (including the cooking) and hired the many cooks who have continued to maintain and build Blueberry Hill's fine food tradition.

Today, Blueberry Hill is reputed to be one of the nation's premier country inns and cross-country ski touring centers. I have a lot of people to thank. I think this book recognizes many of them.

THE
BLUEBERRY HILL
COOKS

Here's to the Blueberry Hill cooks—those talented men and women who brought not only their culinary expertise but their individual life experiences to their tenures at the inn. Collectively, they have developed a cuisine of style and flair, a repertoire of delicious recipes that is uniquely Blueberry Hill.

Some have moved on from Blueberry Hill, but remain in the food/restaurant field; others have taken up new careers, or returned to former occupations. (One, Arlyn Hertz, is the guiding force behind this cookbook.) All, however, are fondly remembered in the inn's folklore and traditions.

Now, let's call the roll. Here are the contributing cooks, in chronological order, with a *Where are they now?* update:

1971–present	*Tony Clark*	Still proprietor, and still lending a hand with the cooking when needed.
September 76–March 80; August 89–present	*Elsie Sherrill*	Elsie was pastry chef at another Vermont inn for a while, but now has returned to the Blueberry Hill family.
June 81–March 82	*Laurie Caswell*	Now a career consultant—and sometime caterer.
December 81–March 82; June 84–October 85	*Lynn Levy*	Has now left the food world and become a Certified Public Accountant.
April 82–March 83	*Tory Sneff*	Manages a restaurant in Fairfax, Virginia.
September 82–April 84	*Irene Eilers*	A potter—with her studio in the Blacksmith Shop at Blueberry Hill.
December 82–April 84	*Laurie Taylor*	Still in Vermont, in the produce business.
May 84–October 84	*Jeanne Eliades*	Jeanne now owns a hotel and restaurant in California, but still finds time to cook.

June 84–October 85	*Alan Levy*	Al and his wife, Lynn (see above), met and married at Blueberry Hill. Al is now a consultant in the computer industry.
December 85–November 86	*Arlyn Hertz*	Now at the M.I.T. Center for Space Research in Cambridge, Massachusetts
January 86–January 88	*Donna Kerr*	Still baking in Middlebury, Vermont
October 86–present	*Shari Brown*	From cooking and baking at Blueberry Hill Shari has moved on to become our gardener, producing the edible flowers that garnish many Blueberry Hill dishes.
December 86–October 88	*Fran McDermott*	This "Chef de Cuisine" degree holder is now cooking in the Boston area.
April 88–September 88	*Adria Lagasse*	Now working part-time in the food and catering business, as well as in the nursing profession.
August 88–present	*Diana Mooney–Van de Velde*	Diana now finds herself running the kitchen at Blueberry Hill—quite a change from the sailing ships she cooked on for 2½ years.

You'll find out more about these cooks as you read through this book, for we've included bits of their personal histories and comments with each recipe. (You'll also note, as you read these comments, that occasionally a recipe was originated by one cook but submitted, with attribution and thanks, by another—a demonstration of the spirit of sharing that has developed among Blueberry Hill cooks over the years.) And don't be fooled by the fact that some of these cooks stayed at Blueberry Hill for only a year, or a season; each of them made a deep impression on the inn's collective cuisine, and their contributions will be remembered as long as there is a Blueberry Hill.

To those who created the memorable dishes in this book, and those to come in the future: we thank you for your skill and imagination, and we salute you all!

BREAKFAST

❦
Orange Almond Pancakes

If you think the buck stops at blueberry pancakes—think again. This recipe, and the following one for raspberry pancakes with honey butter, both show what a little imagination and interesting additions can do for ordinary pancakes. — *Alan Levy*

SERVES 4

¼ cup milk
½ cup fresh orange juice
2 tablespoons melted sweet butter
1 egg yolk
2 tablespoons freshly grated orange rind
1 cup unbleached white flour
2 teaspoons baking powder
2 tablespoons sugar
½ teaspoon salt
½ cup slivered almonds, lightly toasted
1 egg white
Maple syrup
Butter

1. In a medium bowl, combine the milk, orange juice, melted butter, egg yolk, and orange rind. Set aside.
2. In a large bowl, mix together the flour, baking powder, sugar, and salt.
3. Slowly add the milk mixture to the flour mixture, stirring gently with a fork until just combined. Stir in the almonds.
4. Beat the egg white until stiff and fold it into the combined mixture.
5. Ladle the batter onto a lightly greased hot skillet or griddle to form 3-inch circles. Cook until bubbles form, flip, and cook until golden brown, about 1 minute.
6. Serve with butter and heated Vermont maple syrup.

RASPBERRY PANCAKES
WITH HONEY BUTTER

— Alan Levy

SERVES 4

¾ cup milk

2 tablespoons melted sweet butter

1 egg yolk

1 cup unbleached white flour

2 teaspoons baking powder

2 tablespoons sugar

½ teaspoon salt

1 egg white

1 cup fresh raspberries, picked over and washed

1 stick (8 tablespoons) sweet butter

2 tablespoons honey

Maple syrup (optional)

1. In a medium bowl, combine the milk, melted butter, and egg yolk. Set aside.
2. In a large bowl, mix together the flour, baking powder, sugar, and salt.
3. Slowly add the milk mixture to the flour mixture, stirring gently with a fork until just combined.
4. Beat the egg white until it is stiff and fold it into the combined mixture, then fold in the raspberries.
5. Before cooking the pancakes, prepare the honey butter. Whip the butter with the honey until fluffy. Put it in a pastry bag and set aside in a cool place until ready to use. (Note that 1 stick of butter plus 2 tablespoons honey will make *more* than enough for 1 recipe of pancakes.)
6. Ladle the batter onto a lightly greased griddle or skillet to form 3-inch circles. Cook until bubbles form, flip, and cook until golden brown, about 1 minute.
7. Pipe the honey butter onto the hot pancakes and serve with a pitcher of warm Vermont maple syrup.

BLUEBERRY HILL
WILD BLUEBERRY PANCAKES

This was and continues to be the most-requested breakfast entrée, as attested by the many "blue" smiles of guests leaving the dining room. Serve them up with Country Apple Sausage (see recipe on page 19) for a truly Vermont-style breakfast. — *Laurie Taylor*

SERVES 4

1¼ cups unbleached white flour
1 tablespoon sugar
1 tablespoon baking powder
½ teaspoon salt
4 eggs, separated
2 cups milk
¼ cup sweet butter, melted
1 cup wild blueberries, rinsed and picked over
Butter
Maple syrup

1. In a large mixing bowl, mix together all the dry ingredients. Set aside.
2. Lightly beat the egg yolks, then add the milk and melted butter and mix well. Set aside.
3. Beat the egg whites until they form stiff—but not dry—peaks. Set aside.
4. Make a hollow in the center of the dry ingredients. Pour in the milk mixture and blend batter well. Don't worry about a few lumps—they will work themselves out.
5. Carefully fold in the egg whites until well incorporated. Gently stir in the blueberries.
6. Ladle the batter onto a lightly greased hot skillet or griddle to form 3-inch circles. Cook till bubbles form, flip, and cook until golden brown, about 1 minute.
7. Serve with butter and heated Vermont maple syrup.

❧
POTATO PANCAKES
WITH CHUNKY APPLE-PEAR SAUCE

I remember wonderful Sunday mornings at home, reading the paper while the great aroma of hearty potato pancakes filled the house. My family served them as a prelude to going sailing, but at the inn they hit the spot equally well with guests stoking up for a long day of skiing. Just remember, the apple-pear sauce should be prepared either the evening before or well enough ahead of time so that it has a chance to chill. — *Irene C. Eilers*

SERVES 4 TO 6

Apple-Pear Sauce

3 Granny Smith apples

3 pears

Grated rind of 1 orange

Juice of 1 orange

1 to 2 tablespoons Vermont maple syrup (optional)

½ teaspoon cardamom

Pinch of cinnamon

Potato Pancakes

2 cups grated mature potatoes (not "new")

3 eggs

1½ tablespoons unbleached white flour

Salt to taste

Freshly grated nutmeg to taste

2 tablespoons grated onion

1 tablespoon salad oil

4 tablespoons salad oil

1. To prepare the sauce: peel and core the apples and pears and cut them into chunks. Place them in a medium saucepan with the grated rind, orange juice, and maple syrup, if desired. Sprinkle in the cardamom and the cinnamon.

2. Cover and simmer gently, stirring occasionally until the fruit begins to fall apart but some chunks remain. If more cooking liquid is needed, add more orange juice. When the fruit is cooked, adjust the flavoring to your liking.

3. Let the sauce cool, then refrigerate in a covered bowl until serving time.

4. To prepare the pancakes, peel and coarsely grate the potatoes. Squeeze out as much moisture as possible, either in a colander or a muslin towel.
5. Beat the eggs and add them to the potatoes. Add the flour, salt, nutmeg, onion, and 1 tablespoon oil.
6. Place the 4 tablespoons of oil in a heavy skillet over medium-high heat. Depending on the consistency of the batter, either shape it into rounds about ¼ inch thick and 3 inches in diameter, or ladle directly onto the heated skillet. Sauté the pancakes on one side until brown and crisp, then turn to brown and crisp the other side.
7. Serve the pancakes piping hot out of the pan with a large spoonful of the slightly chilled chunky apple-pear sauce.

❦
Puffed Pancakes

This is a nice alternative to traditional pancakes. Try to serve the dish immediately from the oven, so your guests can appreciate the soufflé-like effect.
— *Arlyn Hertz*

SERVES 4

4 eggs
1 cup flour
1 cup milk
1 teaspoon vanilla extract
Dash salt
2 tablespoons granulated sugar
5 tablespoons sweet butter
¼ teaspoon cinnamon
Confectioners' sugar
Maple syrup

1. Preheat oven to 425°.
2. In a blender or food processor fitted with a steel blade, mix the eggs, flour, milk, vanilla, salt, and sugar until smooth.
3. Melt the butter in a 9-inch Pyrex pie dish in the oven until it sizzles. Do not let the butter brown.
4. Remove the baking dish from the oven and immediately pour the batter into the sizzling butter. Sprinkle with the cinnamon.
5. Bake in the middle of the oven for 20 minutes, or until puffed and brown. Serve immediately with confectioners' sugar and warm maple syrup.

LUCY'S FABULOUS BAKED FRENCH TOAST

Lucy was right: this *is* fabulous! And having some on hand in your freezer means you're always ready to serve up a special breakfast without any notice or preparation. — *Arlyn Hertz*

SERVES 4

> 4 eggs
> ¾ cup milk
> ¼ cup light cream
> 2 tablespoons sugar
> 1 teaspoon vanilla extract
> ¼ teaspoon freshly ground nutmeg
> 1 tablespoon brandy (optional)
> 8 slices day-old French bread, cut ¾-inch thick
> 6 tablespoons melted butter
> Cinnamon-sugar
> Maple syrup

1. In a food processor fitted with a steel blade, blend all the ingredients except the bread and the butter.
2. Place the bread in one snug layer in a shallow baking dish.
3. Pour the liquid over the bread and let it sit a few minutes. Turn the slices over and let them soak up the rest of the liquid.
4. Freeze the bread uncovered overnight (or until frozen). Once it is frozen, it can be packed in an airtight container or plastic bag and returned to the freezer until ready to use.
5. To cook, preheat the oven to 475°. Lightly butter a baking sheet.
6. Place the frozen bread on the baking sheet. Brush each slice generously with the melted butter.
7. Bake in the oven for 10 minutes. Turn the bread over and brush each slice with more melted butter. Return to the oven and bake another 8 to 10 minutes, or until it is nicely browned.
8. Dust the toast lightly with confectioners' sugar. Serve with a bowl of cinnamon-sugar and a pitcher of warm maple syrup.

❦
Blueberry Hill
Granola

A guest at the inn described this crunchy treat as "scrumptuliosis." The recipe is simple and basic and easily improvised upon once you get the knack. In fact, no one cook devised this particular mix—it's evolved over the years. This makes a hefty batch but it goes fast. Keep it stored in an airtight container and it will keep for weeks. — *Arlyn Hertz*

MAKES ABOUT 18 CUPS

> 2 quarts rolled oats
> 2 cups each sesame seeds, sunflower seeds, chopped walnuts, and sliced almonds
> 1 to 2 cups dark brown sugar, depending on desired sweetness
> 1 tablespoon cinnamon
> 1 tablespoon nutmeg (optional)
> 1 cup wheat germ (optional)
> ½ pound sweet butter, melted
> 1 tablespoon vanilla extract
> 2 cups raisins

1. Preheat the oven to 300°.
2. In a super large bowl, mix together all the dry ingredients except the raisins. Pour on the melted butter and the vanilla and continue to stir until everything is well blended.
3. Transfer granola to two large cookie sheets or shallow baking pans and spread evenly.
4. Toast granola for 45 minutes, stirring every 15 minutes. Turn off oven and let granola cool in the oven with the door open. When cool, stir in the raisins, then put in an airtight container to store.

❦
Stewed Winter Fruit

All stewed fruit is not created equal, as this recipe proves. It's a wonderful warm way to start a winter morning, or make this breakfast treat part of an elegant dessert by spooning it (warm) over vanilla ice cream. — *Arlyn Hertz*

SERVES 20 OR MORE

1 pound dried apricots

1 pound pitted dried prunes

1 pound pitted dried dates

1 pound currants

1 pound coarsely chopped pecans or walnuts

4 apples, cored and cubed

4 pears, cored and cubed

¾ cup maple syrup

1 cup apple cider

Heavy cream

1. Preheat the oven to 375°.
2. In a large casserole dish, layer the dried fruits, nuts, and fresh fruit.
3. Pour the maple syrup and apple cider over the fruits.
4. Cover tightly and bake for 1 hour and 15 minutes, or until the fruits are soft.
5. Serve warm with a pitcher of heavy cream.

Fresh Fruit
with Yogurt Sauce

This simple dish is based on childhood memories of wonderful, carefree summer days when it seemed my greatest worry was to pick the same number of strawberries as my brother for this favorite treat of ours. You can serve it as a breakfast fruit dish, over granola, or as a summer treat any time of day.

— *Irene C. Eilers*

SERVES 4

1 cup plain yogurt

¼ cup maple syrup *or* honey *or* brown sugar (or to taste)

1 teaspoon vanilla extract

¼ teaspoon ground cardamom

2 tablespoons freshly grated orange rind

1 cup heavy cream, whipped to soft peaks

2 cups (or more) of fresh seasonal fruit, washed and sliced

Fresh mint sprigs

1. Combine the yogurt, sweetener, vanilla, cardamom, and orange rind. Stir well, and adjust seasonings and balance of ingredients to taste. Fold the whipped cream gently into the yogurt mixture.
2. Add the fresh fruit to the yogurt mixture just before serving. Mix lightly and divide evenly among 4 small bowls. Garnish with a sprig of fresh mint.

❧

TONY'S FRENCH OMELET

One of my first summer jobs was working the "omelet line" at a holiday resort in England. Since then many, many omelets have been served at Blueberry Hill, especially during the early days of Breadloaf Summer School when Sunday night was omelet night at the inn—simple and easy, with so many variations. Here is my favorite. I suggest using a copper pan, if you have one, for a true "French" touch. (And we of course use brown New England eggs.)

— Tony Clark

SERVES 1

> 2 extra large eggs
> 2 tablespoons heavy cream
> Salt and freshly ground black pepper to taste
> 2 tablespoons sweet butter
> ½ cup chopped avocado
> ½ cup chopped Canadian smoked ham
> ¼ cup crumbled Montrachet goat cheese
> Watercress

1. Heat a 6-inch pan (copper or other) with 1 tablespoon of butter. Use medium, not high, heat.
2. In a small bowl, mix the eggs well. Add the heavy cream, salt, and pepper, and mix again.
3. Add the remaining tablespoon of butter to the pan. It should sizzle, but not brown.
4. Add the egg mixture to the pan, off the heat. Aerate the mixture about a half-dozen times with a fork.
5. Return the pan to the heat and add the avocado, ham and cheese, spreading well. If necessary, continue to cook until eggs are set.
6. Using a spatula, roll omelet onto itself by turning both sides towards the center. Flip the omelet, seam-side down, onto a warmed plate.
7. Garnish with watercress.

❦
BAKED EGGS FLORENTINE

This is a nice breakfast or brunch dish, especially suitable for a crowd since you won't have to cook eggs individually on top of the stove. — *Jeanne Eliades*

SERVES 4

> 1 12-ounce bag of spinach, washed and drained
> 1 medium yellow onion, chopped fine
> 2 tablespoons sweet butter
> 2 tablespoons olive oil
> 1 cup grated Swiss cheese
> 4 extra-large eggs at room temperature
> Salt and freshly ground black pepper to taste
> Toast or English muffins

1. Preheat the oven to 375°. Butter an 8-inch-square baking pan.
2. Trim the stems off the spinach and tear the leaves into small pieces.
3. In a large skillet, heat the butter and olive oil over medium heat. Place the onion in the pan and sauté briefly. Add the spinach and cook, tossing with a large wooden spoon until the spinach is wilted. Remove from the heat and let cool. Drain the spinach in a colander and discard the liquid.
4. Spread the spinach evenly in the prepared baking pan. Sprinkle with the cheese. Crack the eggs individually into a small bowl and slide onto the spinach-cheese bed, being careful not to break the yolks. Space the eggs evenly in the pan. Salt and pepper generously.
5. Bake for 10 to 15 minutes, or until the whites of the eggs are completely set. Divide into 4 equal servings and serve with toast or English muffins.

❦
OVERNIGHT CHEESE SOUFFLÉ

This is an easy breakfast treat that lets the cook sleep a few extra winks—or, if necessary, run outside to help round up the inn's three pigs when they break loose! — *Laurie Caswell*

SERVES 8

12 slices of bread, crust removed, cubed

1 pound grated cheese, mixture of Swiss and cheddar

8 eggs

4 cups half and half

1¼ teaspoons dry mustard

1 teaspoon salt

1. The night before serving, butter a 13½-by-8¾-inch glass baking pan.

2. Sprinkle the bread cubes evenly over the bottom of the pan. Spread the grated cheese over the bread.

3. In a blender, mix the remaining ingredients. Pour the liquid over the bread and cheese. Cover and refrigerate overnight.

4. When ready to serve, remove the baking pan from the refrigerator and bring it to room temperature. Preheat the oven to 350°.

5. Bake uncovered for 1 hour, or until puffed and lightly browned. Serve immediately.

❦
BAKED EGGS
WITH EXPLORATEUR CHEESE

Explorateur cheese is a triple-cream cheese similar to double-cream Brie, but much milder. Vary this recipe simply by trying different cheese and herb combinations. — *Arlyn Hertz*

SERVES 1

2 eggs

1 one-inch cube of Explorateur cheese

1 tablespoon (total) of finely chopped chives, scallions, and parsley

1 tablespoon heavy cream

Salt and freshly ground black pepper

1. Preheat oven to 400°. Lightly butter a 3-inch ramekin.

2. Toss the Explorateur in the herbs and place in the ramekin. Break the eggs carefully over the cheese and drizzle the cream over the eggs. Sprinkle with salt and pepper to taste.

3. Place the ramekin in a baking pan and pour boiling water into the pan to come 1 inch up the side of the ramekin.

4. Bake about 20 minutes, depending on how firm you prefer the eggs. Serve immediately.

❦

COUNTRY APPLE SAUSAGE

Make a special breakfast even more special by presenting these sausages baked with apples. They're easy to serve to a crowd, as you can prepare them ahead of time just to the point when you'd put them in the oven. Another bonus is the drippings—they're delicious, and can be used to baste other meats.

— Laurie Caswell

SERVES 4

> 4 large sweet Italian pork sausages
> ⅓ cup Vermont maple syrup
> 3 Cortland apples, cored and cut into wedges

1. Preheat the oven to 400°.
2. In a heavy skillet, with no fat added, sauté the sausages over medium to high heat until brown. Transfer the sausages to a small baking dish, cover them with the apple wedges, and drizzle with the maple syrup.
3. Cover and bake for 10 minutes. Decrease the temperature to 350° and continue baking until done, about 15 to 20 minutes. (The apples should not fall apart.)

MUFFINS
&
COFFEECAKES

Apple Walnut Muffins

I associate these moist, apple-studded muffins with crisp fall mornings at Blueberry Hill: apple season has begun, I have finally run out of blueberries, and these muffins celebrate both those events. These moist muffins keep well without being frozen. — *Lynn Levy*

MAKES 24 SMALL OR 16 LARGE MUFFINS

>1 cup sweet butter at room temperature
>2 cups sugar
>3 eggs
>1 tablespoon cinnamon
>3 teaspoons vanilla extract
>3 medium apples, finely chopped
>2 cups chopped walnuts
>1 cup raisins
>1½ teaspoons baking soda
>½ teaspoon salt
>3 cups unbleached white flour

1. Preheat the oven to 325° and oil the muffin tins.
2. In a large mixing bowl, thoroughly cream the butter, sugar, and eggs. Add the cinnamon, vanilla, apples, walnuts, and raisins, and mix until combined.
3. In a separate bowl, sift together the flour, baking soda, and salt. Blend these into the batter (it will be stiff).
4. Spoon the batter into the oiled muffin tins. (Fill ⅔ full for small muffins, to top for large.) Bake for 25 minutes, or until a toothpick comes out clean when inserted into the center of a muffin.

Blueberry Muffins

A classic at Blueberry Hill. — *Arlyn Hertz*

MAKES 12 MUFFINS

>6 tablespoons sweet butter at room temperature
>1½ cups sugar

2 eggs

2 cups unbleached white flour

¼ teaspoon salt

2 teaspoons baking powder

½ cup milk

1 teaspoon vanilla extract

2 cups blueberries, picked over, washed, and well drained

3 tablespoons sugar mixed with 1 teaspoon cinnamon

1. Preheat the oven to 375°. Grease the top and insides of muffin pans.
2. In a large bowl, cream the butter and 1½ cups sugar until light and fluffy. Add the eggs one at a time, mixing well between each.
3. Sift together the flour, salt, and baking powder. Add this alternately in thirds with the milk to the creamed mixture. Add the vanilla.
4. Crush ½ cup of the blueberries with a fork and add to the batter (stirring by hand—do not use a beater). Add the remaining 1½ cups of whole berries and stir gently.
5. Fill the muffin tins to the top with the batter. Top each muffin with a sprinkle of the cinnamon-sugar.
6. Bake for 30 minutes. Turn off the oven and leave the muffins in the oven for another 20 minutes. (If using an electric oven, turn off the heat and open the door.)

❦
CURRANT SCONES

This is my all-time favorite pastry—not too sweet and perfect served with butter and homemade blueberry jam. — *Jeanne Eliades*

SERVES 6

2 cups unbleached white flour

1 tablespoon baking powder

2 tablespoons sugar

½ teaspoon salt

⅓ cup sweet butter

¼ cup currants

Grated rind from 1 orange

1 egg
⅔ cup half and half
1 egg yolk plus 1 tablespoon water, mixed
Cinnamon-sugar

1. Preheat oven to 425°.
2. Mix flour, baking powder, sugar, and salt together in a large mixing bowl.
3. Using a pastry blender or fork, cut in the butter until the mixture resembles coarse meal.
4. Stir in the currants and orange rind.
5. In a separate bowl, beat the egg lightly with a fork. Slowly beat in the half and half. Add this mixture to the dry ingredients and combine thoroughly.
6. Pat the dough into a flat circle, about 6 to 8 inches in diameter, then cut it into 6 pie-shaped wedges. Brush the tops with the egg yolk and water mixture, then sprinkle with the cinnamon-sugar.
7. Place wedges on an ungreased baking sheet, sides *not* touching, and bake for 10 to 15 minutes, until brown on top. Serve warm from the oven!

❦
BLUEBERRY BANANA NUT TEA LOAF

This became a great summertime coffee cake because there were always ripe bananas in the fruit bowl and plenty of blueberries waiting to be picked, with 200 bushes just outside the kitchen door. — *Elsie Sherrill*

MAKES ONE 9-INCH LOAF

1 cup blueberries, picked over and washed
2 tablespoons unbleached white flour
2 eggs, lightly beaten
⅓ cup sweet butter
1 cup mashed ripe banana
1½ cups unbleached white flour
⅔ cup sugar
2¼ teaspoons baking powder

½ teaspoon salt

¼ teaspoon cinnamon

⅔ cup rolled oats

½ cup chopped walnuts

¼ cup raisins

1. Preheat oven to 350°. Butter a 9-inch loaf pan.
2. Toss the blueberries with the 2 tablespoons of flour and set aside.
3. In a large mixing bowl, cream the eggs, butter and banana.
4. In another bowl, combine the 1½ cups flour, sugar, baking powder, salt, cinnamon, and rolled oats. Stir this, a little bit at a time, into the creamed mixture and continue to stir until the batter is well combined.
5. Stir in the nuts and raisins.
6. Place the batter in the prepared loaf pan and bake for 50 minutes, or until a toothpick inserted in the center of the loaf comes out clean.
7. Remove from the oven and cool in the pan on a rack for 15 minutes.

❧

BLUEBERRY COFFEE CAKE

Blueberry coffee cake is symbolic of the country-fresh flavor of the inn. The guests help by picking the blueberries from the cultivated bushes in the backyard. Don't let the presence of mashed potatoes scare you away from baking this coffee cake; they add a special flavor and texture. — *Tory Sneff*

MAKES ONE 13½-BY-8¾-INCH CAKE

Cake

2 cups sifted unbleached white flour

2 teaspoons baking powder

1 cup sweet butter at room temperature

2 teaspoons orange extract

1 teaspoon grated orange peel

2 cups sugar

4 egg yolks

1 cup mashed potatoes, cooled to room temperature

4 egg whites

¾ teaspoon salt

2 cups blueberries, washed and picked over

2 tablespoons flour

———

Orange Cream Icing

> 1 cup confectioners' sugar
>
> 1 tablespoon sweet butter, softened
>
> 1 teaspoon grated orange peel
>
> 1 teaspoon light corn syrup
>
> 2 tablespoons sour cream

1. Preheat oven to 350°. Grease and flour a 13½-by-8¾-inch shallow baking pan.
2. Blend the 2 cups of flour and baking powder. Set aside.
3. Cream together the butter, orange extract, and orange peel. Add the sugar gradually, beating vigorously. Add the egg yolks, one at a time, beating well after each addition. Mix in the mashed potatoes.
4. Add the dry ingredients in thirds, beating only until blended after each addition.
5. Beat the egg whites and salt until stiff, not dry, peaks are formed. Gently fold into the batter.
6. Dredge the blueberries with the 2 tablespoons of flour. Fold the berries into the batter carefully. Turn into the prepared pan and bake for 35 to 40 minutes.
7. Cool in baking dish on a wire rack.
8. Prepare the icing: combine all the ingredients and beat until smooth. Spread evenly over the cooled cake.

❦

GERMAN HONEY-ALMOND COFFEE CAKE

A moist, rich, and wonderfully gooey breakfast treat. — *Arlyn Hertz*

SERVES 8

> ½ cup ricotta cheese
>
> 4 tablespoons milk
>
> 4 tablespoons vegetable oil
>
> ¼ cup sugar
>
> Dash of salt
>
> 2 teaspoons baking powder
>
> 1½ cups unbleached white flour

5 tablespoons sweet butter

¼ cup sugar

⅓ cup honey

1 cup sliced almonds

1 teaspoon vanilla extract

1. Preheat the oven to 350°. Butter the bottom of a 9-inch springform pan. Set aside.
2. In a large bowl, mix the cheese, milk, oil, ¼ cup sugar, and salt.
3. Sift the baking powder with the flour and add to the wet mixture. Stir well and then knead lightly for about 5 minutes to form a smooth ball. Set aside for 10 minutes.
4. To prepare the topping: melt the butter in a heavy saucepan. Add the sugar and honey and stir constantly over medium heat until the mixture is thick and coats a wooden spoon. Add the almonds. Remove from the heat and add the vanilla.
5. Pat the dough into the prepared springform pan. Spread the topping over it.
6. Bake 25 to 30 minutes, making sure the topping doesn't get too brown. Let the cake cool 5 minutes, then remove the sides of the pan. Serve warm.

❦

FAVORITE COFFEE CAKE

I really like making this coffee cake—it's *so* easy, and you can vary it by simply changing the toppings. — *Donna Kerr*

SERVES 8 TO 10

Cake

1½ cups unbleached white flour

¾ cup sugar

2½ teaspoons baking powder

¾ teaspoon salt

¼ cup salad oil

¾ cup milk

1 egg

Topping

⅓ cup brown sugar

¼ cup unbleached white flour

½ teaspoon cinnamon

3 tablespoons cold sweet butter

1. Preheat oven to 375°. Grease a round 9-inch cake pan or an 8-inch-square pan.
2. In a large mixing bowl, blend the dry ingredients for the cake. Add the oil, milk, and egg and beat vigorously for 1 minute. Spread in the prepared pan.
3. Prepare the topping: combine all the ingredients with a fork until the mixture has the consistency of breadcrumbs.
4. Sprinkle the topping evenly over the cake batter. Bake 25 to 30 minutes, or until a wooden pick inserted in the center comes out dry and clean. Serve warm.

BREADS

SUNFLOWER MILLET BREAD

Simply, it's the greatest bread—somewhat earthy, but enjoyed by all. A perfect example of the plain, wholesome foods I prefer. — *Lynn Levy*

MAKES 2 LOAVES

2¼ cups lukewarm water
⅝ cup vegetable oil
½ cup honey
2½ tablespoons dry yeast
3 cups whole-wheat flour
3½ cups unbleached white flour
1½ tablespoons salt
½ cup rolled oats
¼ cup hulled millet
¼ cup hulled sunflower seeds

1. In a large mixing bowl, combine the lukewarm water, oil, and honey. Stir until the honey is dissolved.
2. Sprinkle the yeast into the mixture, stirring constantly until dissolved. Allow to sit undisturbed for about 10 minutes.
3. After the yeast has risen to the surface and become foamy, mix in half of the flour. Beat the batter until it develops a glossy, elastic texture. Cover the dough with a warm cloth and allow it to rest in a warm place until doubled, about 20 minutes.
4. Stir down the dough until it is about its original size. Add the salt, oats, sunflower seeds, and millet and stir until they are well incorporated into the dough.
5. Gradually add the remaining flour until the dough becomes too stiff to stir. Turn it onto a floured board and knead for 10 minutes, adding more flour as necessary. The dough should remain moist, but not sticky; firm, but not dry.
6. Oil the dough and return it to the bowl. Cover with a damp cloth and let it rise again in a warm place until it has doubled in size.
7. Punch the dough down, turn out on a floured surface, and knead for about 5 minutes. Cut the dough in half and shape each half into a loaf. Place the loaves in lightly oiled bread pans and let rise until slightly more than double.
8. Preheat the oven to 350°. Bake about 40 minutes or until a loaf sounds hollow when tapped on the bottom. Remove the loaves from the pans and cool on a wire rack.

GRANOLA BREAD

I found this recipe years ago on a cereal box. The only change I made was to use homemade granola (see page 14 for the Blueberry Hill Granola recipe). This is the best bread recipe I have, and it makes delicious sandwiches.

— *Tory Sneff*

MAKES 2 LOAVES

6½ cups unbleached white flour

2 packages yeast

1 tablespoon salt

1¼ cups water

1 cup milk

½ cup honey

¼ cup oil

2 cups homemade granola (without any dried fruit), crushed

2 eggs

1. In a large mixing bowl, combine 3 cups flour, yeast, and salt. Mix well.
2. In a small saucepan, heat the water, milk, honey, and oil until warm, 120 to 130 degrees. Add to the flour mixture.
3. Add the eggs and blend at low speed until moistened.
4. By hand, gradually stir in the granola and enough of the remaining flour to make a firm dough. Knead on a floured surface until smooth and elastic, about 10 minutes.
5. Place the dough in a greased bowl, turning to grease the top. Cover with a damp cloth and let rise in a warm place until doubled, about 1½ hours.
6. Punch the dough down. Divide into 2 parts, then divide each part into 3 pieces. Roll each piece out by hand to make a 14-inch rope. Place ropes side by side, pinch them together at one end, and braid loosely. Pinch ends and tuck under to seal. Repeat with other half of dough.
7. Place each loaf in a greased 9-by-5-inch loaf pan. Cover and let rise in a warm place until light and doubled, about 1 hour.
8. Preheat the oven to 375°. Bake the bread for 30 minutes or until golden brown. (If it browns too fast, cover loaves loosely with foil for the last 5 to 10 minutes of baking.)
9. Immediately remove loaves from pans and cool on wire racks.

Four o'Clock
Sesame French Bread

Like clockwork, each afternoon at four I began making sesame French bread so it would be just out of the oven and piping hot for dinner at eight.

— *Laurie Taylor*

MAKES 3 LOAVES

> 1 tablespoon sweet butter
> 1 tablespoon salt
> 1 tablespoon sugar
> 2 cups boiling water
> 1 tablespoon dry yeast
> ⅔ cup lukewarm water
> 6 to 6½ cups unbleached white flour
> 1 cup toasted sesame seeds
> ¼ to ½ cup yellow cornmeal

1. In a large mixing bowl, combine the butter, salt, sugar, and boiling water. Stir to dissolve the ingredients and let cool to lukewarm.
2. In another bowl, sprinkle the yeast over the ⅔ cup lukewarm water. Let the yeast dissolve and start to foam. Add the yeast mixture to the first liquid mixture.
3. Mix together the flour and sesame seeds. Slowly add the flour mixture to the liquids, beating well after each addition. When well combined, turn dough out on a floured board and knead until it is smooth and elastic.
4. Form the dough into a ball and place in an oiled ceramic or earthenware bowl. Cover it with a damp cloth and place in a warm spot. Let the dough rise for 1 to 1½ hours, or until double in size.
5. Punch the dough down, knead into a ball, return to the bowl, cover, and let rise again 1 hour or until double in size.
6. Preheat the oven to 400°. Brush 3 French bread pans with oil and sprinkle the bottoms with cornmeal. (If you don't have special pans, use a large cookie sheet and prepare with oil and cornmeal.)
7. Punch the dough down and divide it into 3 parts. Shape each loaf by patting it into a rectangular shape, then rolling it tightly into a long loaf. Pinch the seam and ends to seal. Place the loaves seam-side down in pans or on cookie sheet.

8. Cover the loaves with the damp cloth and let rise until doubled, about 30 minutes.

9. Bake the loaves on the middle rack of the preheated oven for about 1 hour. For a crisp, hard crust, brush the loaves often with cold water.

10. Serve the bread warm from the oven with lots of fresh sweet butter.

❧

CRUSTY FRENCH BREAD

This is the first bread I learned to do. It's basic and easy and the dough is great to work with. It's also a great bread for any occasion. And save the leftovers —they're great for homemade croutons or french toast. — *Donna Kerr*

MAKES 4 LOAVES

> 7 to 8 cups unsifted unbleached white flour
> 1 teaspoon sugar
> 1 tablespoon salt
> 3 tablespoons (or packages) of dry active yeast
> 3 tablespoons softened sweet butter
> 2½ cups of very warm tap water (120 to 130 degrees)
> Cornmeal

1. In a large bowl, thoroughly mix 2½ cups of flour with the sugar, salt, and undissolved yeast. Add the softened butter and mix well.

2. Gradually add the tap water to the dry ingredients. Beat the mixture with an electric mixer set to medium speed for about 2 minutes, scraping the sides of the bowl often.

3. Add another cup of flour and beat on high speed for 2 minutes. Stir in enough additional flour to make a stiff dough. Turn out on a lightly floured surface and knead a few times. Form the dough into a ball.

4. Lightly oil a large bowl and place the dough in it. Cover with plastic wrap and put it in a warm place. Let the dough rise for about 2 hours or until it is doubled in bulk.

5. Punch the dough down one time. Divide the dough into 4 equal pieces. Shape each piece into a 15-by-8-inch oblong, then roll it up in a long, thin loaf.

6. Place the loaves on greased sheets that have been sprinkled with cornmeal. Let them rise in a warm place until doubled in bulk, about 20 to 25 minutes.

7. Preheat oven to 450°. With a sharp knife, make about 5 slashes across the top of each loaf. Bake the loaves for about 25 minutes. During the baking, spray the loaves with water 3 or 4 times, to ensure a nice hard crust.

8. Loaves are done when crust is nicely brown and a hollow sound is made when you tap the bottom of the loaf.

❦

CHIVE-BASIL BREAD

If you're lucky enough to have fresh herbs growing outside your back door (or on your kitchen windowsill), try this aromatic bread. And don't feel limited to using chives and basil—add or substitute your own favorites. I've made it with rosemary and chives, and it's wonderful. — *Donna Kerr*

MAKES 1 LARGE LOAF

> 1 tablespoon dry yeast
> ½ cup warm water
> 1 egg, lightly beaten
> ½ teaspoon salt
> 3 tablespoons sweet butter, melted
> ½ cup finely chopped fresh chives
> ¼ cup finely chopped fresh basil
> 3 cups unbleached white flour

1. In a large mixing bowl, dissolve the yeast in the warm water. Stir in the egg, salt, butter, chives, and basil.

2. Beat in the flour, 1 cup at a time, to form a stiff dough.

3. Turn the dough out onto a floured board and knead about 10 minutes, or until smooth and elastic. Place the dough in a buttered bowl, rotate it so all surfaces are greased, and cover loosely with a damp cloth. Let dough rise in a warm place until doubled in bulk.

4. Punch dough down, shape into a loaf and place in a greased 9-inch loaf pan. Cover and let rise again until it has doubled in size.

5. Preheat the oven to 350°. Place loaf in preheated oven and bake for 50 minutes. Bread is done when it is lightly brown on top and the bottom makes a hollow sound when you thump it with your fingers.

6. Cool bread on a wire rack, or, better yet, serve warm with lots of sweet butter.

HEARTY
WHOLE WHEAT BREAD

Monica Sanchez, a former baker at Blueberry Hill, was instrumental in teaching me the basics of bread baking. I inherited this recipe from her, experimented, and came up with my own variation, lighter than the original but still earthy and hearty—definitely not for the "squishy bread" crowd.

— *Donna Kerr*

MAKES 2 LOAVES

2 tablespoons dry yeast
½ cup warm water
2 cups low-fat milk
3 tablespoons sweet butter
2 tablespoons molasses
1½ teaspoons salt
3½ cups unbleached white flour
2½ cups whole-wheat flour
½ cup wheat germ

1. Dissolve the yeast in the warm water and set aside.
2. In a small saucepan, warm the milk just enough to dissolve the butter, then stir in the molasses and the salt.
3. In a large mixing bowl, combine 2 cups of the unbleached white flour with the whole-wheat flour and wheat germ. Save the rest of the white flour for flouring the board and your hands while kneading.
4. Stir in the yeast and warm milk mixture and blend thoroughly. Turn the dough out onto a floured board and knead for about 15 minutes, or until dough is smooth and elastic. Place dough in a greased bowl, rotate dough so all the surfaces are greased, then cover with a damp cloth. Let dough rise in a warm place until it is doubled in bulk.
5. Punch dough down, knead for 1 minute, then shape into 2 loaves. Place each loaf in a greased 9-inch loaf pan, cover each with a damp cloth, and let rise again just until the dough rises over the top of the pan.
6. Preheat the oven to 425°. Bake the loaves for 10 minutes, then reduce the heat to 400° and bake for another 25 minutes or until the loaves make a hollow sound when thumped on the bottom with your fingers. Cool loaves on wire racks.

DILL-CARAWAY DINNER ROLLS

Elsie Sherrill, another cook at Blueberry Hill, taught me this recipe. It's a really moist dough, easy to work with, and I recommend it for beginners. If you don't fancy rolls, you can divide the dough into two loaves and bake them in greased 9-inch loaf pans for about 40 minutes. — *Donna Kerr*

MAKES ABOUT 30 ROLLS

> 3 cups cottage cheese
> 3 tablespoons sweet butter, melted
> ½ cup minced onion
> 3 tablespoons dry yeast
> 1½ cups warm water
> 7 cups unbleached white flour
> ¼ cup sugar
> 2 teaspoons salt
> 3 eggs, at room temperature
> 2 tablespoons caraway seeds
> 3 tablespoons dill weed

1. In a small pan, heat the cottage cheese until warm. Set aside.
2. In another small pan, sauté the onion in the butter until it is soft and translucent. Add this to the cottage cheese.
3. Stir the yeast into the warm water and wait until it gets foamy.
4. In a large bowl, combine the flour, salt, and sugar. Add the yeast and stir well.
5. Add the eggs, one at a time, stirring well after each addition, then stir in the caraway and dill. The dough will be moist.
6. Lastly, add the cottage cheese and onions and stir until all the ingredients are well combined.
7. Turn dough onto a well-floured board and knead lightly for 5 minutes.
8. Place the dough in a greased bowl, cover loosely with plastic wrap, and let rise in a warm place until doubled in size.
9. Punch the dough down and form into rolls—about 30—or two loaves, if desired. Place rolls about 2 inches apart on a greased cookie sheet (or loaves in bread pans) and allow to rest for about 15 minutes. They will rise slightly.
10. While the rolls are resting, preheat the oven to 350°. Bake rolls 15 to 20 minutes, bread 45 to 50 minutes.

HORS
D'OEUVRES

❧
Salmon Mousse

This delicate hors d'oeuvre or appetizer is perfect for the most elegant of occasions. — *Tory Sneff*

SERVES 12

> 1 envelope unflavored gelatin
> ¼ cup cold water
> ½ cup boiling water
> ½ cup mayonnaise
> 1 tablespoon freshly squeezed lemon juice
> 1 tablespoon onion, finely grated
> ¼ teaspoon paprika
> 1 teaspoon salt
> 2 tablespoons fresh dill, chopped fine
> 2 cups flaked poached fresh salmon
> 1 cup heavy cream

1. In a large mixing bowl, soften the gelatin in the cold water. Slowly stir in the boiling water and whisk the mixture until the gelatin is dissolved. Let cool.
2. Stir in the mayonnaise, lemon juice, grated onion, paprika, salt, and chopped dill. Blend completely and refrigerate for 30 minutes, or until the mixture begins to thicken slightly.
3. Fold in the finely flaked salmon.
4. In a separate chilled bowl, whip the cream until it thickens to medium peaks. Gently fold the cream into the salmon mixture.
5. Transfer the mixture to a decorative mold. Cover and chill for 4 to 6 hours. Carefully unmold onto a platter.
6. Garnish with watercress and serve with thinly sliced black bread.

❧
Smoked Fish Pâté

This pâté is simple to prepare and even easier to eat! For variation in texture and color, after processing the pâté stir in some finely minced red pepper and red onion. — *Arlyn Hertz*

SERVES 4 TO 6

½ pound smoked fish (either bluefish or trout)

3 ounces cream cheese, at room temperature

3 tablespoons unsalted butter, at room temperature

1 teaspoon white horseradish

1 tablespoon mayonnaise

2 drops Tabasco or other hot pepper sauce

1. Remove the skin and any bones from the fish.
2. Blend the fish and the remaining ingredients in a food processor fitted with a steel blade. Blend until well combined, but don't overprocess. Serve with crackers or thinly sliced dark pumpernickel.

❦
CRUSTLESS CRAB QUICHE

This is a lighter and simpler-to-prepare alternative to traditional crusted quiches. It's also an easy recipe to make substitutions in—try using diced ham instead of crabmeat, or cheddar cheese instead of Monterey Jack.

— *Arlyn Hertz*

SERVES 8

4 eggs

1 cup dairy sour cream

1 cup small-curd cottage cheese

¾ cup grated Parmesan cheese

¼ cup unbleached white flour

⅛ teaspoon salt

4 drops Tabasco or other hot pepper sauce

⅛ teaspoon freshly ground nutmeg

2 cups shredded Monterey Jack cheese

¾ cup diced fresh crabmeat

1. Preheat the oven to 350°. Lightly grease a 10-inch glass pie plate.
2. In a food processor fitted with a metal blade, blend the eggs, sour cream, cottage cheese, Parmesan cheese, flour, salt, Tabasco sauce, and nutmeg.
3. Pour the mixture into a large bowl and stir in the crabmeat and Monterey Jack cheese.
4. Pour into the prepared pie plate and bake for 45 minutes to 1 hour, or until puffed and golden brown and a knife inserted near the center comes out clean. Let the quiche stand for 10 minutes before slicing and serving.

❧
Mussels Steamed in White Wine with Garlic

I served this at the inn as a hearty first course, with plenty of crusty French bread for dunking. However, it also makes a perfect main course when served with lots of French bread and a simple Caesar salad (see recipe on page 58).
— *Laurie Taylor*

SERVES 8

> 10 pounds fresh mussels
> 6 cups dry white wine (please use something good enough
>   to drink)
> ¼ pound sweet butter
> ½ teaspoon white pepper
> 1 tablespoon olive oil
> 2 tablespoons minced scallions
> 2 bulbs garlic (yes, 20 cloves in all)
> ½ cup fresh parsley, chopped

1. To clean the mussels, soak and rinse them three times in cold water to rid them of sand. Pull the "beards" off. If a mussel is partially open and has no reflex closing reaction when thumped on the edge of the sink, it is dead and should not be eaten.
2. Place the cleaned mussels in a large pot. Add the wine, butter, white pepper, olive oil, scallions, garlic, and ¼ cup of parsley. Bring to a gentle boil and steam until the mussels open, about 15 minutes.
3. To serve, ladle mussels and broth into warm soup bowls and sprinkle with remaining parsley. Make sure there is lots of broth in each bowl for dipping crusty French bread.

❧
Olive Anchovy Dip

This quick and easy hors d'oeuvre spread is perfect on pumpernickel, or, for a more elegant presentation, use a pastry bag and pipe it decoratively onto cucumber rounds. — *Frances McDermott*

SERVES 6

8 ounces cream cheese, at room temperature

2 tablespoons anchovy paste

¼ cup pitted Greek olives

½ small red onion

1. Put all the ingredients in the bowl of a food processor fitted with a steel blade. Process until smooth.
2. Transfer to a serving bowl and refrigerate until ready to serve.

SHRIMP TARTLETS

Individual tartlets make a delicate first course. If you don't have small tart pans, partially bake the pie crust in a 9-inch quiche pan. Follow the recipe to prepare the filling, then bake for about 35 minutes. — *Lynn Levy*

SERVES 8

Pastry for a 9-inch piecrust (see recipe on page 155)

1½ cups medium shrimp, peeled, deveined, and cut in half

½ cup chopped green onion

1 tablespoon sweet butter

½ pound Gruyère or Fontina cheese, grated

1 cup mayonnaise

4 eggs

1 cup half and half

½ teaspoon salt

½ teaspoon dill weed or 1 tablespoon minced fresh dill

1. Preheat the oven to 400°.
2. Divide the pastry into 8 small balls. Roll out each piece in a circle and press into the 8 small tartlet pans. Trim the edges and set aside in the refrigerator while preparing the filling.
3. Sauté the shrimp and green onion in the butter until the shrimp just turn pink. Spread evenly over the bottom of each tartlet pan.
4. Distribute the grated cheese evenly over the shrimp.
5. Beat together the mayonnaise, eggs, half and half, salt, and dill weed. Pour over the mixture in the tartlet pans.
6. Bake the tartlets for 15 to 20 minutes. Remove them from the oven, let them sit for 5 minutes, then carefully remove them from their pans and serve immediately.

ASIAN SHRIMP AND PASTA

This is a colorful dish that's a treat to the palate with a highly spiced sauce featuring ginger, garlic, and red pepper flakes. It makes a great first course, side dish at a barbecue, or luncheon entrée. — *Arlyn Hertz*

SERVES 10 TO 12

¾ cup peanut oil
2 inches ginger root, finely minced
2 cloves garlic, finely minced
¼ teaspoon red pepper flakes, or to taste
½ cup soy sauce
2 tablespoons rice-wine vinegar
½ pound Chinese buckwheat noodles or linguine
½ pound spinach linguine
½ pound snow peas, washed and destringed
3 carrots, peeled
2 scallions, chopped
1 pound medium shrimp, cleaned and cooked

1. In a small saucepan, heat the oil with the ginger. When the oil begins to bubble, remove pan from the heat and add the garlic and red pepper flakes. Cool to room temperature. When cool, add the soy sauce and rice-wine vinegar. Stir well and store overnight (or longer) in a nonreactive container at room temperature.

2. Bring a large pot of water to a full boil. Add a pinch of salt and the buckwheat noodles and boil for about 8 minutes or until *al dente*. Rinse the noodles well with cold water and drain. Set aside in a large bowl. Repeat this procedure for the spinach linguine and add it to the buckwheat noodles.

3. Julienne the carrots into ⅛-by-2-inch strips. Set aside.

4. Julienne the snow peas into ⅛-by-2-inch strips. Set aside.

5. Bring a large pot of water to a boil. Blanch the carrots for 45 seconds, then plunge them into cold water and drain well. Blanch the snow peas for 20 seconds, plunge them into cold water and drain well.

6. Add the vegetables and the shrimp to the pastas, then pour on the ginger-garlic-pepper sauce. Toss well. Cover and refrigerate. When ready to use, remove pasta from the refrigerator and bring to room temperature. Toss well again before serving.

DOMESTIC BOURSIN-STYLE CHEESE

This spread is simple to prepare in a food processor or blender, and we think it tastes better than the store-bought "real thing." — *Tory Sneff*

MAKES ABOUT 1 CUP

> 1 8-ounce package cream cheese at room temperature
> ½ cup sweet butter at room temperature
> 1 teaspoon minced garlic
> 4 tablespoons freshly grated Parmesan cheese
> 2 tablespoons white wine
> 2 tablespoons freshly minced parsley
> ½ teaspoon dried thyme leaves
> ½ teaspoon marjoram

1. Combine all the ingredients in a food processor fitted with a steel blade or in a blender. Blend until thoroughly mixed and smooth.
2. Scrape into a small bowl and refrigerate until serving.
3. Serve with crackers or party pumpernickel.

BAKED BRIE

I made this appetizer when I was a guest at Blueberry Hill. It's simple, delicious, and impressive—and it got me the job as cook! — *Arlyn Hertz*

SERVES 8

> 1 pound firm brie at room temperature, rind removed
> 3 cloves garlic, minced
> 2 tablespoons cognac
> ¼ teaspoon dried tarragon

1. Preheat the oven to 350°.
2. In a medium bowl, mash the brie, garlic, cognac, and tarragon with a fork. When soft and well blended, place in a bake-and-serve crock.
3. Bake for 20 to 25 minutes or until hot and bubbly. Serve with apple and pear slices as well as crackers.

Individual Cheese Soufflés

Timing is critical in serving this light first course. You want to rush these to the table as soon as they emerge from the oven, so they arrive puffed and golden. Serving 25 soufflés before they fell was a tricky business at the inn. Needless to say, much credit was given to whoever was waiting table that evening.

— Lynn Levy

SERVES 6

> 3 tablespoons butter
> 3 tablespoons unbleached white flour
> 2 teaspoons dry mustard
> 1¼ cups milk, scalded and still hot
> 1½ cups grated cheddar cheese (packed, not loose)
> ½ teaspoon salt
> Freshly ground black pepper to taste
> ½ cup chopped fresh chives
> 6 eggs, separated and at room temperature

1. Preheat the oven to 375°. Lightly grease 6 half-cup-size ramekins.

2. In a saucepan, melt the butter. Sprinkle in the flour and the dry mustard, whisking constantly as you sprinkle. Cook this roux for 2 minutes.

3. Slowly add the hot milk to the roux, whisking vigorously during each addition so that the mixture stays smooth and uniform. Cook this sauce over low heat for 8 to 10 minutes, stirring occasionally. Remove from the heat, stir in the cheese, and season with the salt, pepper, and chives. Allow mixture to come to room temperature, stirring every now and then as it cools.

4. Whisk the egg yolks lightly and beat them into the cooled cheese mixture.

5. Beat the egg whites until they are stiff. Quickly fold them into the cheese mixture.

6. Pour the mixture into the 6 prepared ramekins and bake, undisturbed, until they puff up and turn golden brown, about 20 minutes.

7. Serve immediately.

❦
GOAT CHEESE TART

The goat cheese in this recipe provides a mild tang to the filling, which is nicely balanced by the flavor of the fresh herbs. — *Frances McDermott*

SERVES 8

> 1 unbaked prepared tart shell (pâte brisée) pressed into a
>   10-inch pie plate (see recipe on page 156)
> 1 pound soft goat's cheese (Boucheron or Chèvre)
> ¾ cup ricotta cheese
> 2 tablespoons minced fresh garlic
> 3 tablespoons chopped fresh rosemary
> 3 tablespoons chopped fresh thyme
> 3 egg yolks
> Salt and freshly ground black pepper to taste

1. Preheat the oven to 425°.
2. "Blind bake" the tart crust, i.e., line it with aluminum foil and weight it with rice or pie weights. Bake for 7 to 8 minutes and remove from the oven. Remove the foil and weights.
3. Lower the oven temperature to 350°.
4. In a food processor fitted with a steel blade, process the goat cheese, ricotta, garlic, 1 tablespoon rosemary, and 1 tablespoon thyme. Add the egg yolks one at a time. Season with salt and pepper. Process until the mixture is well combined.
5. Pour the mixture into the semi-baked tart shell and sprinkle with the remaining herbs. Bake until slightly puffed and solidified, about 30 minutes. Serve warm.

❦
CÈPES À LA BORDELAISE
(WILD MUSHROOMS)

Having lived in Bordeaux for part of my life, I remember harvesting wild mushrooms on a Sunday afternoon with my mom and dad. Talk about eating some freshness from heaven! This appetizer brings back those memories, especially when served with a good Bordeaux wine. — *Tony Clark*

SERVES 6

1 pound cèpes, chanterelles, morels, shiitake, or other
   wild mushrooms
6 tablespoons sweet butter
1 clove garlic, minced
2 tablespoons fresh parsley, finely chopped
1 bunch watercress, washed and patted dry, for undergarnish

1. Wash, drain, and dry the mushrooms. Remove any tough ends from their stems. Cut them in thick slices.
2. In a large heavy skillet, heat the butter over medium-high heat. Add the mushrooms and sauté for two minutes. (You do not want to overcook them.)
3. Add the garlic and parsley and quickly sauté another minute.
4. Serve immediately on a bed of watercress.

STUFFED MUSHROOM CAPS

This is a great appetizer. It's quite simple and looks smashing presented on a scallop shell or a nasturtium or grape leaf. — *Tony Clark*

SERVES 4

12 large mushrooms
2 tablespoons olive oil
8 maple-smoked sausages or other smoked sausage
1 tablespoon garlic, minced fine
2 tablespoons chopped onions or scallions
Salt and freshly ground black pepper to taste

1. Preheat the oven to 350°.
2. Clean and destem the mushrooms. (Save the stems for another recipe or the stock pot.) Rub the outsides lightly with the olive oil and place on a baking sheet. Set aside.
3. Place the sausage on a baking sheet lined with parchment paper and bake them for 20 minutes.
4. Place the cooked sausage, garlic, onions or scallions, salt, and pepper in a food processor fitted with a steel blade. Pulse until the mixture is finely minced but not puréed.
5. Stuff the mushroom caps with the mixture and bake them in the oven for about 15 minutes.

❧
BAKED ARTICHOKE DIP

I've never seen such an overwhelming response to such a simple recipe. When asked *What is it?*, I would always ponder how I was going to make it sound more complicated. It's definitely a favorite at Blueberry Hill during the cocktail hour. — *Laurie Caswell*

SERVES 8

> 1 16-ounce can artichoke hearts in water, drained
> 1 cup mayonnaise
> 1 cup freshly grated Parmesan cheese
> ½ cup sliced almonds

1. Preheat the oven to 350°.
2. In a food processor fitted with a steel blade, blend the artichokes, mayonnaise, and cheese. Place in a bake-and-serve shallow baking dish and sprinkle with the sliced almonds.
3. Bake for approximately 20 minutes, or until heated through. Serve with crackers or tortilla chips.

❧
ARTICHOKES
WITH LEMON-TARRAGON DRESSING

This makes a great appetizer or salad course for any special dinner. The Dijon-style mustard gives an added zip to the lemon-tarragon dressing—or feel free to substitute your own favorite creamy vinaigrette. — *Laurie Taylor*

SERVES 4

> 4 medium artichokes
> Juice of 1 lemon
> 1 egg
> 2 egg yolks
> ¼ cup tarragon vinegar
> 1 teaspoon dried tarragon leaves
> 1 tablespoon fresh lemon juice
> 1 tablespoon Dijon-style mustard
> ⅛ teaspoon salt

1 good grinding of fresh white pepper
1 cup olive oil
½ cup light salad oil

1. Wash the artichokes, trim the stems, and remove any loose outer leaves.
2. Cut approximately 1 inch off the tops, then snip off the sharp leaf tips from the entire artichoke. Brush the cut edges with lemon juice to prevent discoloring.
3. Bring a large kettle of water to a boil. Add the artichokes, cover, and simmer for about 40 to 45 minutes, until a fork can be inserted easily in the stem.
4. Remove the artichokes from the kettle with tongs and carefully place them, inverted, on paper toweling to drain and cool.
5. When cool, remove the center leaves and scoop out the center to create a pocket for the dressing. Refrigerate until ready to use.
6. In a blender or food processor fitted with a steel blade, combine the egg, egg yolks, vinegar, lemon juice, tarragon, salt, white pepper, and mustard. Blend for 1 minute.
7. With blender or processor running, gradually add the oils, stopping when necessary to scrape down the sides. Refrigerate in a covered jar until ready to use.
8. To serve, spoon ¼ cup of the lemon-tarragon dressing into the center pocket of each artichoke. Place the artichokes on a bed of bib lettuce or endive leaves.

❦

STUFFED LEMONS

I've spent many wonderful days visiting Tony, Chris, and Tim at Blueberry Hill. I've gardened, tinkered, puttered, sewn, and helped out in the kitchen. Although I never acted as "the cook" per se, I thought this special recipe would be a nice addition to a special book. It makes an elegant and delicious first course. — *Mary Clark (Grandma Mary)*

SERVES 4

4 large lemons
6 tablespoons fresh lemon juice

7 ounces sardines, drained of any oil
6 ounces cream cheese
6 tablespoons sour cream
½ teaspoon Dijon mustard
1 green onion, finely minced
⅛ teaspoon paprika
Pinch of cayenne
Salt and freshly ground black pepper to taste
1 egg white
4 large green leaf lettuce leaves, for undergarnish
Fresh thyme for garnish

1. Cut the tops off the lemons and reserve. Carefully scoop out the insides of the lemons (a grapefruit spoon with serrated edges works well) and remove as much pith as possible.
2. In a food processor fitted with a steel blade, process the lemon juice, sardines, cream cheese, sour cream, mustard, onion, and seasonings until smooth. Remove to a large bowl.
3. In a small bowl, beat the egg white until stiff. Fold it carefully into the sardine mixture, making sure ingredients are well combined.
4. Stuff the lemons with the mixture, replace the lemon caps and chill until ready to serve. To serve, place each lemon on a large lettuce leaf and garnish with fresh sprigs of thyme.

FETTUCINE
WITH ASPARAGUS AND FRESH PEAS

This is a lighter cousin to Fettucine Alfredo. It's more colorful, not to mention more digestible. — *Arlyn Hertz*

SERVES 6 TO 8 AS AN APPETIZER

½ pound asparagus, trimmed and cut into 1-inch pieces
1 cup shelled fresh peas
3 tablespoons sweet butter
2 cloves garlic, minced
½ cup diced Westphalian ham

1 pound fettucine

3 eggs

6 tablespoons grated Parmesan cheese

3 tablespoons olive oil

Salt and freshly ground black pepper to taste

1. Blanch the asparagus in boiling water about 1 minute, or until bright green and tender, but still crisp. Immerse it in cold water and drain. Repeat blanching process for the fresh peas. Set aside.

2. In a large skillet, melt the butter over medium heat. Add the garlic and sauté 2 to 3 minutes. Add the ham and sauté 2 minutes. Add the vegetables and sauté a final 2 minutes. Remove from the heat and keep warm.

3. In a large kettle, bring 4 to 5 quarts of salted water to a full boil. Add the fettucine and cook until barely tender.

4. While the pasta is cooking, beat the eggs, salt, pepper, and Parmesan cheese until smooth.

5. Drain the cooked fettucine. Return to the pot and toss with the olive oil.

6. Return the skillet containing the vegetables and ham to the heat, add the fettucine, and toss gently. Add the egg mixture and continue to toss gently until heated through. Serve immediately.

❦

PASTA WITH CITRUS BEURRE BLANC

This is a variation on a classic beurre blanc, stabilized with heavy cream. It's a somewhat lighter alternative to a cream and cheese sauce.

— *Frances McDermott*

SERVES 8

1 pound fresh pasta

⅓ cup minced shallots

½ cup freshly squeezed lemon or orange juice

1 cup dry white wine

2 cups heavy cream

¼ pound sweet butter, cut into small pieces

Salt and freshly ground black pepper to taste

Fresh parsley, minced for garnish

2 scallions, minced for garnish

1. Bring a large kettle of salted water to a full boil. (While waiting for the water to boil, prepare the sauce for the pasta.) When the water is boiling, add the pasta and cook until *al dente*. Drain well.

2. To prepare the sauce, place the shallots, citrus juice, and wine in a small nonreactive saucepan. Cook over medium heat until it is reduced to about 3 tablespoons.

3. Add the heavy cream to the reduction and continue to reduce until there is about 1½ cups and the sauce coats the back of a wooden spoon.

4. Turn off the heat and add the butter, whisked in piece by piece.

5. Strain out the shallots and add the salt and pepper to taste.

6. Serve over the freshly cooked pasta and garnish with fresh parsley and scallions.

❦
SPICY COLD SESAME NOODLES

This is a tasty make-ahead appetizer or side dish. It's great for a crowd—as a matter of fact, I prepared over 10 pounds of it for the inn's traditional ''Pig Race'' (a cross-country ski race followed by a pig barbecue), and there wasn't a noodle left over. — *Arlyn Hertz*

SERVES 10 AS AN APPETIZER

> 1 pound linguine or thin spaghetti
>
> 3 tablespoons peanut oil
>
> ¾ cup sliced radishes
>
> 3 scallions, chopped fine
>
> 3 cloves minced garlic
>
> 1-inch-slice fresh ginger, peeled
>
> 2 teaspoons (or less) crushed red pepper flakes (optional depending on level of spiciness desired)
>
> ½ cup soy sauce
>
> ½ cup rice vinegar
>
> 1 tablespoon sugar or honey
>
> 4 scallions
>
> ¼ cup peanut oil
>
> 3 tablespoons sesame oil
>
> 1 teaspoon hot chili oil (optional)
>
> ½ cup peanut butter or sesame tahini
>
> Lemon zest for garnish
>
> Toasted sesame seeds for garnish

1. In a large kettle, bring 5 quarts of salted water to a full boil. Cook the pasta until *al dente*. Drain well and toss with 3 tablespoons of peanut oil. Set aside in a large bowl with the radishes and 3 finely chopped scallions.

2. In a food processor fitted with a metal blade, combine all the remaining ingredients except the garnishes. Process until very smooth and well blended.

3. Pour the sauce over the noodles and vegetables and toss well. Cover and refrigerate 4 hours. Before serving, toss again and let noodles come to room temperature. Garnish with the toasted sesame seeds and the lemon zest.

❦

TORTELLINI ARLESCO

This makes a wonderful first course or serve it as a side dish at a barbecue. It keeps well, so it can be prepared a day ahead of time. — *Arlyn Hertz*

SERVES 8

> 7 ounces white tortellini
> 7 ounces spinach tortellini
> ¾ cup olive oil
> ¼ cup mild white vinegar
> 2 tablespoons balsamic vinegar
> 3 cloves garlic, finely minced
> 1 cup grated Parmesan cheese
> ½ teaspoon dry mustard
> Salt and freshly grated white pepper to taste
> ¼ teaspoon sugar
> 3 scallions, finely minced
> ½ cup chopped black olives for garnish

1. Bring 4 to 5 quarts salted water to a boil. Cook both kinds of tortellini until firm, about 8 minutes. Drain and rinse well with cold water; drain thoroughly again, then set aside in a large glass bowl.

2. In a medium bowl, mix the olive oil, vinegars, garlic, Parmesan cheese, mustard, salt, pepper, and sugar. Blend well with a fork. Stir in the scallions.

3. Pour the dressing over the pasta and toss well. Cover and refrigerate four hours. Serve garnished with the chopped black olives.

❦
Nachos Christo

Laurie Taylor got me started making nachos when hors d'oeuvres were the only things I knew how to make (I was 12 years old at the time). She gave me the idea, and from there I took off and created this favorite hors d'oeuvre. The vegetables listed are not the only ones you can use—if something looks good, put it in. (That's how I got started!) Even now, every time I make this something different goes in the pan. — *Chris Clark*

SERVES 10

> 1 medium green zucchini, minced
> 1 medium yellow squash, minced
> 1 red pepper, minced
> 1 green pepper, minced
> 2 medium tomatoes, minced
> 1 Bermuda onion, minced
> ½ cup of your favorite salsa (or use the recipe on page 153)
> 1 teaspoon cumin, or to taste
> Nachos chips, enough to cover the pan you use
> 2 cups grated Monterey Jack or cheddar cheese

1. Put all the vegetables and the salsa in a large frying pan and simmer until everything is crisp-cooked, not mushy. Season with the cumin.
2. Spread the nachos over a cookie sheet so no part of the sheet is showing. Cover the nachos with the vegetables and then sprinkle with the grated cheese. Place under the broiler and broil until the cheese is melted. Served hot straight from the oven.

QUESADILLAS

This is a great hors d'oeuvre, especially because it's easy and fast to prepare. I used to make quesadillas for lunch, too, when Hazel and Helena (our wonderful housekeepers) needed a little sustenance after a hard morning.

— Jeanne Eliades

SERVES 6

> 4 flour tortillas
> 1 cup grated Monterey Jack cheese
> 2 green onions, chopped fine
> 1 jalapeño chili, seeded and chopped fine
> Butter for frying
> ¼ cup salsa cruda (see recipe on page 153)
> ⅓ cup sour cream
> 1 avocado, peeled and sliced thin lengthwise

1. Lay 2 tortillas flat, side by side. Divide cheese between the 2 and spread it evenly. Sprinkle each tortilla with the green onions and the jalapeño chili. (If you don't like "hot and spicy" food, you might want to eliminate the jalapeño, or use it sparingly to taste.) Top with the remaining tortillas and press down to flatten.

2. In a large skillet, melt 2 tablespoons butter over medium-high heat. When butter sizzles, place one quesadilla in the pan and cook until it is lightly browned. Flip over to the other side and finish cooking. Transfer the quesadilla to a warm plate. Add more butter to the pan and cook the remaining quesadilla the same way.

3. Cut each quesadilla into 6 wedges. Arrange wedges attractively on a round serving plate and in the center top with the salsa cruda, then sour cream and finally the avocado slices.

EVOLUTIONARY TABOULI

The basics of this recipe have been with me since the sixties, when Americans discovered the joys of different grains and combining "exotic" flavors. Since then this wonderful dish has changed as much as I have, and continues to delight a wide spectrum of people on occasions ranging from a casual picnic to a country wedding. — *Irene C. Eilers*

SERVES 4

1½ cups water
1½ cups bulgar or cracked wheat
1 cup chopped fresh parsley
1 large tomato, coarsely chopped
½ cup chopped fresh mint
1 clove garlic
1½ teaspoons Dijon mustard
Pinch of sugar
1 tablespoon soy sauce
Juice of ½ lemon
¼ cup balsamic vinegar
½ cup olive oil
1 teaspoon cumin (or more)
1 teaspoon cinnamon (or more)

1. In a large saucepan, bring the water to a boil; add the bulgar, cover, and turn off the heat and let it sit undisturbed until cooled.
2. Toss together the tomatoes, parsley, and mint and set aside.
3. Meanwhile, prepare the dressing. Crush the garlic in a garlic press. Mix it with the mustard and sugar, then add the soy sauce, lemon juice, vinegar, and oil. Mix well and set aside.
4. When the bulgar has cooled, put it into a bowl large enough to hold all the ingredients. Fluff it up with a fork and add generous amounts of the cumin and cinnamon. (Bulgar has a way of soaking up flavor and making it disappear!) Toss the bulgar in the dressing and let it sit at room temperature for about 1 hour.
5. Add the tomato-parsley-mint mixture and chill for 1 hour or more. Taste and re-season just before serving—I often end up adding more lemon juice and spices. Serve with wedges of pita bread.

SALADS
&
SALAD DRESSINGS

🍒

GREEN SALAD
WITH WARM CHÈVRE DRESSING

The warm goat cheese dressing, combined with the cold crisp greens, gives this salad an interesting taste and texture. It's a special recipe at Blueberry Hill, but don't wait for a special occasion to try it. With a loaf of warm, crusty French bread, it makes an excellent light dinner. — *Lynn Levy*

SERVES 6

> 8 ounces mild Chèvre or Montrachet cheese, softened
> ⅔ cup light olive oil
> 3 tablespoons finely chopped mixed fresh herbs (try basil, parsley, tarragon, and chives)
> 1 to 2 tablespoons fresh lemon juice
> 8 cups mixed greens (watercress, Boston and bibb lettuces) washed, dried, and broken into bite-size pieces

1. Preheat the oven to 375°.
2. Press the Chèvre into an even layer over the bottom of an ovenproof dish. Pour the oil over the cheese, then sprinkle on the herbs. Bake until the cheese is melted and soft enough to blend easily with the oil, about 15 minutes.
3. Remove the dish from the oven and beat the contents with a fork, adding the lemon juice to taste, until blended.
4. Place the greens in a large bowl, pour the warm dressing over, and toss well.
5. Serve immediately—while the dressing is still warm.

🍒

CAESAR SALAD

This "anchovyless" Caesar salad gets its tang from blue cheese rather than from conventional—but controversial—anchovies. If you're feeling ambitious, garnish the salad with homemade pumpernickel croutons. — *Arlyn Hertz*

SERVES 6 TO 8

¾ cup olive oil

3 cloves garlic, minced fine

4 tablespoons fresh lemon juice

1 tablespoon Worcestershire sauce

⅛ teaspoon salt

¼ teaspoon freshly ground black pepper

1 large head Romaine lettuce, washed, drained, and torn into
  bite-size pieces

1 raw egg, lightly beaten

½ cup crumbled blue cheese

½ cup grated Parmesan cheese

Croutons for garnish

1. In a small glass bowl, mix together the olive oil and the garlic. Let
   them sit for 30 minutes. Add the lemon juice, Worcestershire sauce,
   salt, and pepper, and blend well with a fork. Let the dressing rest for
   another 30 minutes. Mix again with a fork.

2. Place the lettuce leaves in a large salad bowl. Pour on the dressing and
   toss well. Add the raw egg, blue cheese, and Parmesan cheese. Toss
   again. Serve the salad on chilled salad plates and garnish with croutons.

❦
FENNEL SALAD

This salad is a great introduction to the delicate taste of fennel. — *Arlyn Hertz*

SERVES 4 TO 6

3 large fennel bulbs, trimmed and washed

1 cucumber, peeled and thinly sliced

Salt

1 cup red radishes, thinly sliced

2 scallions, trimmed and finely minced

3 tablespoons fresh lemon juice

1 teaspoon sugar

1 tablespoon Dijon mustard

¾ cup olive oil

Salt and freshly ground black pepper to taste

1 cup alfalfa sprouts for garnish

1. Cut the fennel into very thin slices. Place them in a large salad bowl and set aside.

2. Place the cucumber slices in a colander and lightly salt them. Let them drain for 30 minutes. Dry the slices on a paper towel. Add the cucumber slices, radish slices, and minced scallions to the fennel.

3. In a small glass bowl, combine the lemon juice, sugar, Dijon mustard, olive oil, salt, and pepper. Whisk well until creamy.

4. Pour the dressing over the salad and toss well. Cover and refrigerate at least one hour. Serve garnished with alfalfa sprouts.

❦

AVOCADO AND PAPAYA SALAD

This simple little salad is delicious any time of year, provided both the avocado and the papaya are ripe. — *Irene C. Eilers*

SERVES 4

1 avocado, ripe but firm
1 papaya, ripe but firm
1 bunch arugula or watercress
1 head butter lettuce or 1 large endive
Juice of ½ lemon
Juice of ½ lime
2 tablespoons olive oil
¼ teaspoon Dijon mustard
Salt to taste
Pinch of sugar
Freshly ground white pepper to taste

1. Cut the avocado in half, remove the pit, cut into wedges, and remove the peel. Sprinkle with a little of the lemon juice (to prevent it turning brown) and set aside.

2. Cut the papaya in half, scoop out the seeds and stringy parts with a teaspoon, cut into wedges, and remove the peel. Set aside with the avocado.

3. Wash the arugula or watercress and remove any thick stems. Break into bite-size pieces. Wash the lettuce or endive.

4. Prepare the dressing in a large jar: combine the remaining lemon juice, lime juice, olive oil, mustard, salt, sugar, and pepper. Shake well.

5. On individual chilled salad plates, arrange a whole lettuce leaf or three endive leaves. Next, create a nestlike effect with the arugula or watercress to hold alternating wedges of avocado and papaya. Lightly sprinkle with the dressing.

❦

SPINACH AND GOAT CHEESE SALAD WITH BASIL VINAIGRETTE

Goat cheese is my favorite cheese, and one that I have enjoyed on many picnics in France. This classic spinach salad combines my cheese favorite with my herb favorite, basil. — *Tony Clark*

SERVES 6

> 2 12-ounce bags of spinach or equivalent in fresh loose spinach greens
> 6 tablespoons olive oil
> 2 tablespoons red wine vinegar
> Salt and freshly ground black pepper to taste
> ¼ cup fresh chopped basil leaves
> 8 slices bacon, cooked until crisp, drained and broken into small pieces
> 1 pound crumbled Montrachet cheese or "Vermont Chèvre" (an excellent local goat cheese made in Guilford)
> ¼ cup chopped fresh chives

1. Wash, drain, and damp-dry the spinach. Remove the stems and break into bite-size pieces. Set aside in a large salad bowl.
2. Combine the olive oil, vinegar, salt, pepper, and basil leaves in a small bowl. Mix well with a fork and set the vinaigrette aside.
3. When ready to serve the salad, toss the spinach with the basil vinaigrette. Add the bacon pieces and toss again. Divide the salad among the chilled salad plates.
4. Top each plate with crumbled Chèvre, then sprinkle with chives.

❧
SUMMER BEAN SALAD
WITH RASPBERRY VINAIGRETTE

Make this salad when beans are summer fresh, young and tender.

— Laurie Taylor

SERVES 8

2 pounds fresh green beans
1 small red onion, finely chopped
⅓ cup raspberry vinegar
1 tablespoon fresh lemon juice
¼ teaspoon Dijon mustard
⅔ cup virgin olive oil
Salt and freshly ground black pepper to taste
3 tablespoons chopped fresh dill, for garnish

1. Rinse and stem the beans, but leave them whole. Steam them over boiling water until barely tender, only about 7 minutes (a bit longer if beans are more mature). Remove the beans from the steamer and spread them in a thin layer on a large platter. Sprinkle with the chopped onion.

2. Blend together the vinegar, lemon juice, mustard, olive oil, salt, and pepper. Pour the vinaigrette over the warm beans, cover lightly with plastic wrap, and refrigerate for at least one hour. Stir the beans occasionally to ensure that they are well coated with the dressing.

3. Serve the chilled beans garnished with fresh chopped dill.

❧
ROASTED PEPPER SALAD

The secret to this salad is slow-cooking the peppers over low heat. The peppers will be sweet and tender, and, served at room temperature, make a nice alternative to the usual salad of crisp greens. To get the full effect of the colors, serve the peppers on white salad plates. *— Tony Clark*

SERVES 8

2 sweet red peppers

2 green peppers

2 yellow peppers

½ cup olive oil

1 tablespoon minced garlic

1 tablespoon fresh minced chives

1 tablespoon fresh minced basil

1 tablespoon fresh minced rosemary

1. Core the peppers, remove the seeds, and remove any membrane. Slice them in thin rounds.
2. Heat the olive oil on low heat in a large, heavy skillet. Add the peppers and garlic and continue to cook over low heat until tender—about 30 minutes—stirring frequently.
3. When tender, toss in the fresh herbs and salt and pepper and stir. Drain off any liquid and serve at room temperature.

CREAMY BLUEBERRY VINAIGRETTE

Here's another great recipe using our abundant blueberry crop. I served it with a salad of mixed greens, thinly sliced cucumbers, and thinly sliced Bermuda onion, topped off with a handful of whole blueberries. — *Alan Levy*

MAKES ABOUT 1 CUP

4 tablespoons Blueberry Champagne Vinegar (see recipe on page 152)

4 tablespoons olive oil

4 tablespoons plain yogurt

¼ cup fresh blueberries, washed and picked over

⅛ teaspoon salt

Freshly ground black pepper to taste

1. Combine all of the ingredients in a food processor fitted with a steel blade. Process until smooth and refrigerate until ready to use.

❦
Dijon Vinaigrette

I always kept a jar of this basic vinaigrette on hand in the refrigerator at the inn. It's a mild dressing that allows your fresh greens, homegrown tomatoes, and other garden-fresh vegetables to take center stage in any salad.

— *Lynn Levy*

MAKES 1 CUP

> 1 tablespoon Dijon mustard
>
> 4 tablespoons red wine vinegar
>
> 1 teaspoon sugar
>
> ½ teaspoon salt
>
> ½ teaspoon freshly ground black pepper
>
> 1 tablespoon each minced fresh parsley and chives
>
> ¾ cup vegetable oil

1. Measure the mustard into a small bowl and whisk in the vinegar, sugar, salt, pepper, and herbs.
2. Continue to whisk the mixture while slowly drizzling in the oil, until it thickens.
3. Whisk again before serving.

❦
Mustard Vinaigrette

This is my favorite vinaigrette—it's uncomplicated, and perfect on any salad.

— *Arlyn Hertz*

MAKES 1 CUP

> 1 tablespoon cold water
>
> 1 teaspoon dry mustard
>
> 2 large cloves garlic, finely minced
>
> 1 teaspoon sugar
>
> ⅛ teaspoon salt
>
> 1 cup olive oil
>
> 4 tablespoons fresh lemon juice

1. Mix the water and dry mustard together in a large glass jar or 2-cup glass measuring cup. Let the mixture sit 15 minutes.

2. Add the remaining ingredients and mix well with a fork or small wire whisk. Let the dressing rest at least 1 hour at room temperature. Mix well again before serving.

☙

Honey Mustard Vinaigrette

Sweet, spicy, and speedy. It's best served on a salad of green leaf lettuce, orange slices, and thinly sliced purple onion. The honey mustard, readily available in specialty food stores and cheese shops, gives the dressing its sweet and pungent nature. — *Frances McDermott*

MAKES 1½ CUPS

> ¼ cup red wine vinegar
> ¾ cup extra virgin olive oil
> 2 tablespoons honey mustard

1. Whisk the olive oil into the vinegar, then whisk in the honey mustard, a tablespoon at a time. That's all there is to it!

☙

Green Goddess Herb Dressing

The fennel seeds in this dressing provide a unique flavor. It's wonderful on a mixed tossed salad of green leaf lettuce, tomatoes, fresh basil leaves, and thinly sliced cucumber. It also makes a delicious dressing for potato salad, especially if you add a handful of fresh dill to the dressing along with the parsley and basil. — *Arlyn Hertz*

MAKES ABOUT 1 CUP

> ¼ cup chopped fresh basil leaves
> ¼ cup chopped fresh parsley
> 1 egg yolk
> 2 tablespoons tarragon vinegar
> ½ teaspoon fennel seed
> ¼ teaspoon salt
> ¾ cup sunflower or salad oil
> 2 tablespoons light cream or milk

1. In a food processor fitted with a steel blade, process the basil leaves, parsley, egg yolk, vinegar, fennel seed, and salt until well combined, about 20 seconds.

2. With the processor running, gradually add the oil. Transfer the mixture to a refrigerator container and stir in the light cream or milk. Add more if you find the consistency too thick. Chill before serving.

❧

POPPY SEED
SALAD DRESSING

This dressing turns plain green lettuce into something special. At the inn, I served it with a salad of red leaf lettuce, sliced avocados, green grapes, and Bermuda onions, and inevitably I was asked for the dressing recipe. I'm sure your guests will compliment you with the same request. — *Arlyn Hertz*

MAKES ABOUT 2½ CUPS

⅔ cup cider vinegar or other high quality fruit vinegar

1 small onion, peeled and quartered

1½ teaspoons salt

2 teaspoons dry mustard

¾ cup granulated sugar

1 cup sunflower or salad oil

¼ cup poppy seeds

1. In a food processor fitted with a steel blade, process the vinegar, onion, salt, mustard, and sugar until smooth. With the processor running, slowly add the oil and continue to process until it is well incorporated.

2. Transfer the dressing to a large jar and stir in the poppy seeds.

SOUPS

Chilled Avocado Soup

This rich, creamy, light-green soup is best served in small portions, well chilled and garnished with spicy tomato salsa, minced cilantro leaves, and tortilla chips. — *Frances McDermott*

SERVES 10

> 3 ripe avocados
> 2 cups heavy cream
> 1 cup milk
> ¼ cup dry sherry
> ½ teaspoon salt, or to taste
> 1 teaspoon ground cumin
> Freshly ground black pepper to taste
> Pinch of cayenne pepper
> ¾ cup minced purple onion
> ½ cup fresh cilantro leaves

1. Peel and pit the avocados. Cut the avocado in pieces and put in the bowl of a food processor fitted with a steel blade.
2. With the processor running, add the cream, milk, and sherry. Stop the machine and add the salt, black pepper, cayenne, onion and cilantro. Turn on the processor and continue to process until smooth and creamy. Chill well before serving.

Cold Strawberry Soup

This is a wonderful summer soup. The deep, rich, pink color is enhanced if you serve it with a rosette of sour cream and a fresh mint sprig on top. Also, try substituting other fresh fruit. I've made this recipe with blueberries, and also with peaches. — *Arlyn Hertz*

SERVES 4 TO 6

3 cups strawberries, washed and hulled

¾ cup sugar

½ cup water

2 tablespoons cornstarch

1 cup freshly squeezed orange juice

1 3-inch cinnamon stick

½ cup port

1½ cups sour cream or yogurt (or any combination of the two)

Sour cream, fresh mint (for garnish)

1. Purée the berries with the sugar and water in a blender or a food processor fitted with a steel blade.
2. Transfer the berries to a large saucepan and simmer over medium heat for 10 minutes.
3. Mix the cornstarch with the orange juice and add it to the strawberries. Add the cinnamon. Simmer till thick.
4. Remove the soup from the heat and let cool completely at room temperature. When cool, whisk in the port and the sour cream or yogurt. Refrigerate the soup until ready to serve. Garnish with sour cream and a sprig of mint.

❧

POTAGE OF MINTED SNAP PEAS AND GREENS

I served this scrumptious fresh garden soup as the first course to a salmon entrée. It includes two of my favorites from the inn gardens: snap peas and fresh-picked mint. — *Tory Sneff*

SERVES 6

6 ounces fresh spinach, washed, de-stemmed, and torn

6 ounces watercress (1 small bunch), washed and stemmed

4 tablespoons sweet butter

2 large yellow onions, finely chopped

3½ cups chicken stock

12 ounces sugar snap peas, de-stringed, rinsed, and patted dry
1 small bunch fresh mint, washed, stemmed, and patted dry
1 cup light cream
Salt and freshly ground black pepper to taste
Additional washed mint leaves for garnish

1. Steam the spinach and watercress until wilted; drain well and squeeze out any excess liquid. Set aside.
2. Melt the butter in a large heavy saucepan over medium heat. Add the chopped onion, cover, and cook over low heat until lightly colored, about 20 minutes.
3. Pour the chicken stock into the onions and stir in the peas, watercress, and spinach. Bring to a boil. Reduce the heat and simmer, partially covered, for about 15 minutes, or until the peas are tender.
4. Add the mint to the pot, cover, and simmer for another 5 minutes.
5. Strain the soup, reserving the liquid. Transfer the solids to the bowl of a food processor fitted with a steel blade. Add 1 cup of the cooking stock and process until smooth.
6. Return the puréed soup to the pot. Add the cream and about one additional cup of the cooking liquid. Add more liquid if soup is too thick.
7. Season to taste with salt and pepper. Simmer gently until the soup is heated through, then serve immediately garnished with additional mint leaves.

❦
LAST-MINUTE CONSOMMÉ

This is one of those simple but great recipes that come about as a result of desperation. It was one of those evenings when I was pressed for everything, especially time, and just forgot about the soup. Fortunately, the ever-present pot of chicken stock reminded me of those wonderfully sparse Japanese soups. This is what I served that evening, but, as in most of my recipes, it was really only the basis for many variations to follow (and perhaps the first time anything resembling "nouvelle cuisine" was served at the inn). — *Irene C. Eilers*

SERVES 4

4 cups chicken stock, skimmed of all fat

½ teaspoon salt *or* ⅛ cup soy sauce

16 steamed cauliflower flowerets

½ cup sliced black olives

4 tablespoons chopped fresh parsley *and/or*
  minced scallion greens

2 tablespoons toasted sesame seeds

Other great additions:

Steamed peapods

Diced tofu

Cooked shrimp

Sliced mushrooms

1. Bring the chicken stock to a strong simmer and season with salt or soy
   sauce. Adjust the seasoning to your taste.
2. Divide the cauliflower, olives, and parsley among 4 soup bowls. Ladle
   in the hot stock. Sprinkle with sesame seeds and serve immediately.

TOMATO BISQUE

The herbs in this recipe work subtly to give this soup a most unusual flavor.
It's smooth and rich, and a great way to use winter tomatoes. For those who
prefer a lighter version, dilute the bisque with 2 more cups of chicken stock
and use light cream instead of heavy. — *Arlyn Hertz*

SERVES 8

½ cup sweet butter

1 cup chopped celery

2 medium onions, chopped

2 medium carrots, chopped

⅓ cup unbleached white flour

3 pounds ripe tomatoes, chopped

1 cup chicken stock

½ cup tomato paste

1 tablespoon sugar

1 teaspoon dried basil

1 teaspoon dried marjoram

1 bay leaf

1 teaspoon paprika

1 teaspoon curry powder

¼ teaspoon white pepper

2 cups heavy cream

Salt to taste

Toasted sesame seeds for garnish

1. Melt the butter in a large heavy saucepan. Sauté the celery, onions, and carrots until tender. Stir in the flour and cook for three minutes over medium heat, stirring constantly. Add the tomatoes and chicken stock and simmer 5 minutes. Remove from the heat and let cool about 20 minutes.

2. Transfer the cooled mixture to a food processor fitted with a metal blade and blend until puréed.

3. Return the purée to the saucepan, add the tomato paste, sugar, basil, marjoram, bay leaf, paprika, curry powder, and pepper. Cover and simmer over low heat for 25 minutes, stirring occasionally.

4. Discard the bay leaf and add the cream. Stir to blend over low heat. Add the salt and continue to stir until the soup is heated through, but never allowed to boil.

5. Serve hot garnished with toasted sesame seeds.

❦

SOUP MARSEILLES

This is my own version of the more complicated French peasant soup, bouillabaise. The broth is rich and aromatic. For a special treat, serve it with freshly baked Four o'Clock Sesame French Bread (see the recipe on page 32).

— *Laurie Taylor*

SERVES 4

2 tablespoons olive oil

1 leek, washed well and coarsely chopped

1 green pepper, seeded, stemmed, and coarsely chopped

4 medium garlic cloves, minced

3 cups mussel broth or fish stock

2 cups fresh plum tomatoes, peeled, seeded, and quartered, *or* 1 can (16 ounces) Italian plum tomatoes

¼ cup red wine

2 tablespoons fresh chopped parsley

2 tablespoons fresh chopped basil

Salt and freshly ground white pepper to taste

2 cups mussel meat (See recipe on page 40 for directions on how to clean and steam mussels. Save the liquid and use as mussel broth in this recipe.)

1. Heat the oil in a large soup pot over low heat. Add the leek, pepper, and garlic and cook until soft. Add the mussel broth or stock, tomatoes, wine, parsley, basil, salt, and pepper. Bring to a boil. Immediately lower the heat to a slow simmer.
2. Add the mussel meat to the slowly simmering soup and simmer for one hour.
3. Serve piping hot with french bread.

❦

Purée of Lentil Soup with Whipped Cream

I always asked my mother to cook lentil soup on my birthday, and it has remained a favorite to this day. My mother's version was a meal in itself. I wanted a first course for the inn, so I took my love for lentil soup and came up with my own recipe which pleased many a guest, even some non–lentil lovers.

— *Irene C. Eilers*

SERVES 6

2 cups lentils, rinsed

7 cups chicken or vegetable stock (more if needed)

3 whole garlic cloves, peeled

1 bay leaf

1 small onion, finely chopped

2 tablespoons olive oil

¼ teaspoon (generous) ground cumin

⅛ teaspoon (scant) ground cinnamon

⅛ teaspoon (scant) curry powder

½ cup white wine

½ cup heavy cream
Salt and freshly ground black pepper to taste
½ cup heavy cream, whipped to soft peaks
½ cup chopped fresh parsley
Pinch of cinnamon for garnish

1. Put rinsed lentils into a large pot and add the stock, garlic, and bay leaf. Cover and bring to a rolling boil, then reduce the heat and let the soup simmer for about 2 hours, or until the lentils are tender.

2. Meanwhile, in a small skillet, sauté the onions in the olive oil until limp. Add the cumin, cinnamon, and curry powder, and sauté another 2 minutes. Add the white wine and deglaze the pan. Cover and simmer another 5 minutes.

3. Remove the bay leaf from the cooked lentils and place half of the lentils in the bowl of a food processor fitted with a steel blade. Add the onion-spice mixture and process until mixture is puréed. Return this to the pot of lentils and raise the heat to medium.

4. Add the ½ cup of heavy cream and enough extra stock to bring the soup to your desired consistency. Adjust the spice seasoning and season with salt and pepper to taste. Stir in the chopped parsley.

5. To serve, ladle the hot soup into bowls and top with a generous tablespoon of whipped cream, then sprinkle lightly with cinnamon.

❦

WINTER TOMATO SOUP

This unusual, rich red soup demonstrates the versatility of tomatoes. When teamed with different herbs and combined with honey, sherry, and cream cheese, the flavor and consistency of the resulting soup is lush, smooth, and aromatic. And it's especially simple to make at the last minute as no stock is required. — *Alan Levy*

SERVES 4

1 tablespoon sweet butter
1½ cups chopped onion
1 clove garlic, minced
3 cups chopped tomatoes
½ teaspoon salt
½ teaspoon dried rosemary
½ teaspoon dried basil

Freshly ground black pepper to taste
4 ounces cream cheese, broken into small pieces
3 tablespoons dry sherry
¼ cup honey
¼ cup fresh chopped parsley, for garnish

1. In a large, heavy saucepan, melt the butter over medium heat. Add the onion and garlic and sauté about 3 minutes. Add the chopped tomatoes, cover, and cook for 20 minutes over low heat.

2. Add the salt, rosemary, basil, and pepper. Increase the heat to medium and cook for 15 minutes, then turn back to low and simmer another 15 minutes. Remove the soup from the heat and let it cool to room temperature.

3. Put the cooled soup in a food processor fitted with a steel blade and process, adding the cream cheese one piece at a time, until the soup is a smooth purée. Return the soup to the saucepan and place over medium heat.

4. Add the honey and sherry and stir until the soup is heated to serving temperature. Serve garnished with fresh parsley.

❦

CREAM OF
WINTER SQUASH SOUP

This is a creamy and rich potage—a wonderful holiday soup that's a great beginning to a feast of turkey or goose. — *Laurie Caswell*

SERVES 8 TO 10

2 large acorn squash *or* one 2-pound butternut squash
4½ cups homemade chicken stock
¼ teaspoon salt
⅛ teaspoon freshly ground white pepper
1½ cups whipping cream
⅛ teaspoon freshly grated nutmeg
⅛ teaspoon cardamom
2 tablespoons dry sherry
Nutmeg for garnish

1. Halve squash and remove the seeds. Cut into 2-inch cubes.

2. Steam the squash for about 30 minutes, or until it can be easily pierced with a fork. Drain and scoop squash pulp from the skin.

3. Place the pulp in a food processor fitted with a steel blade and purée until very smooth.

4. Return the purée to a large saucepan and whisk in the chicken stock, salt, and pepper. Bring the squash mixture to a boil, reduce the heat and simmer, covered, for about 20 minutes.

5. Keeping the heat on low, add 1 cup of the whipping cream, the fresh nutmeg, the cardamom, and the sherry. Stir constantly until heated through.

6. Beat the remaining ½ cup of whipping cream until soft peaks are formed. Ladle the soup into bowls and garnish with a swirl of whipped cream and additional grated nutmeg. Serve immediately.

❦

POTAGE DE VERMONT

This smooth and creamy soup does justice to our wonderful Vermont cheddar cheese. Although I always served it as a first course, it would make a delicious dinner of its own, accompanied by a loaf of crusty bread and a simple salad. — *Laurie Caswell*

SERVES 8

> 2 tablespoons sweet butter
> ½ cup chopped carrots
> ½ cup chopped onion
> ½ cup chopped fresh dill weed
> ½ cup chopped celery
> 5 tablespoons unbleached white flour
> 5 cups chicken stock
> 3 cups grated Vermont cheddar cheese
> 2 cups half and half
> Salt and freshly ground white pepper to taste
> Toasted sesame seeds for garnish

1. Sauté the carrots, onion, dill, and celery in the butter in a large saucepan. Sprinkle in the flour 1 tablespoon at a time, stirring after each addition.

2. Add the stock. Bring to a boil over medium heat, and cook for about 5 minutes. Strain out the vegetables, purée them in a food processor fitted with a steel blade, then return the puréed vegetables to the stock. Continue to cook over medium heat until the soup boils, then reduce the heat and let it simmer slowly for 15 minutes.

3. Add the grated cheese, stirring constantly with a large wire whisk until it is melted. Slowly add the half and half and stir until well blended. Add the salt and pepper to taste. Serve at once garnished with the toasted sesame seeds.

ENTREES

❦
BEEF TENDERLOIN
WITH IRISH WHISKEY SAUCE

This dish is at its best when served rare to medium-rare. The meat will remain very tender and the sauce is a perfect complement. — *Alan Levy*

SERVES 10

>1 5-pound beef tenderloin, at room temperature
>1 tablespoon freshly ground black pepper
>½ pound bacon
>3 tablespoons sweet butter
>½ cup minced shallots
>1 pound sliced mushrooms
>2 cups heavy cream
>⅓ cup Irish whiskey
>Salt and freshly ground black pepper to taste

1. Preheat the oven to 425°.
2. Remove all the fat and silverskin from the tenderloin (easier done when it's still cold), then rub the entire outside of the beef with the pepper.
3. Place the tenderloin in a large baking pan and wrap it with the bacon strips.
4. Roast the beef for 10 minutes, then reduce the heat to 350° and roast another 25 minutes for rare, 35 minutes for medium.
5. Prepare the sauce while the beef is cooking. In a saucepan, melt the butter over medium heat. Add the shallots and sauté until transparent. Add the mushrooms and continue to sauté until they have given up their liquid and the liquid has evaporated.
6. When the mushrooms are fully cooked add the cream and cook until the liquid is reduced to 1 cup. Add the Irish whiskey and continue to cook another 5 minutes. Season with salt and pepper, then remove from the heat and keep warm until ready to serve.
7. Remove the cooked tenderloin from the oven and let it rest for 10 minutes before slicing. To serve, ladle some warm sauce over the tenderloin slices.

❦
BEEF TENDERLOIN
STUFFED WITH
BASIL SHALLOT BUTTER

A tenderloin can be stuffed with any compound butter. Basil is one of my favorite herbs, and seems to complement the beef well. — *Frances McDermott*

SERVES 10

> 1 5-pound tenderloin of beef at room temperature, trimmed of all the fat and silverskin
> 1 pound maple-cured bacon
> 1 pound sweet butter, at room temperature
> 6 to 8 shallots, minced
> 1½ cups fresh basil leaves, finely chopped
> ½ cup dried basil leaves, revived in boiling water and well drained
> Salt and freshly ground white pepper
> Whole basil leaves and cherry tomato halves for garnish

1. Preheat the oven to 425°. Make sure the tenderloin is trimmed of all fat. Separate the bacon into individual strips.
2. In a food processor fitted with a steel blade, cream the butter, shallots, basil, salt, and pepper until well combined.
3. Trim the rounded ends off the tenderloin, but save these end pieces.
4. Insert a long, narrow, sharp chef's knife into one end of the tenderloin and twist the knife to make a hole. Repeat this procedure on the other end so that the hole extends through the center of the entire loin.
5. Put the basil butter in a pastry bag with a large plain tip. Fill the tenderloin with the butter from one end, then the other. Seal on each end with the trimmings you saved. Wrap the entire tenderloin well with the bacon.
6. Place the beef in a large baking pan and roast for 10 minutes. Reduce the heat to 350° and roast for another 25 minutes for rare, 35 minutes for medium.
7. Remove the roast from the oven and let it rest for 10 minutes before slicing. Garnish sliced beef tenderloin with the fresh basil leaves and cherry tomato halves.

STUFFED SCALLOPINI OF VEAL

This is a simple and elegant way to serve veal. You can stuff and roll the veal filets ahead of time and then refrigerate until you're ready to bake them. Just remember to bring the stuffed veal rolls to room temperature before putting them in the oven. — *Diana Mooney–Van de Velde*

SERVES 4

1 tablespoon olive oil
1 medium onion, chopped
½ cup mushrooms, chopped fine
2 shallots, minced
1½ cups ground veal
2 cloves garlic
1 tablespoon fresh thyme, chopped
1 tablespoon fresh parsley, chopped
⅛ teaspoon salt
Freshly ground black pepper to taste
1 egg
¼ cup heavy cream
8 filets of veal, each about ¼ pound and pounded thin
   (⅛- to ¼-inch thick)
8 slices bacon
2 tablespoons olive oil
1 cup red wine
¼ cup butter, chilled

1. Preheat the oven to 350°.
2. Sauté the chopped onion in the olive oil over medium heat until transparent and limp. Remove from the pan and set aside.
3. Add the mushrooms and shallots to the same pan (add a little more olive oil if necessary) and sauté over medium heat until the mushrooms give up their moisture.
4. To prepare the stuffing, place the onions, mushroom mixture, ground veal, garlic, thyme, parsley, salt and pepper, egg, and cream in the bowl of a food processor fitted with a steel blade. Pulse until well combined, being careful not to overprocess and purée the mixture.

5. Place about 3 to 4 tablespoons of the stuffing in the center of each veal filet and roll it up. Wrap each filet with a slice of bacon and secure with toothpicks.

6. Heat the 2 tablespoons of olive oil in a heavy skillet over medium-high heat. Sauté the rolled filets, turning them so they are browned on all sides. Remove the filets and place them in an ungreased baking pan. The filets should fit tightly in one layer. Pour the wine into the pan.

7. Bake the veal, uncovered, for about 10 minutes. Transfer the filets to a warm platter, remove the toothpicks and bacon, and cover them to keep them warm while preparing the sauce.

8. Transfer the wine and juices that the filets cooked in to a heavy saucepan. Place over medium heat and simmer until the wine reduces to about ½ cup. When reduced, whisk in the chilled butter, one tablespoon at a time, and continue to whisk until all the butter is incorporated. Remove from the heat and serve a little sauce over each filet.

Pork Tenderloin Medallions in Vermouth-Mustard Sauce

Pork prepared this way is as tender as beef tenderloin. — *Arlyn Hertz*

SERVES 4 TO 6

> 2 pork tenderloins, each about 1 pound
> Salt and freshly ground black pepper
> 3 tablespoons sweet butter
> 3 tablespoons olive oil
> 2 large cloves garlic, finely minced
> 1 tablespoon grated lemon rind
> 1 cup dry vermouth
> ¼ cup Dijon mustard
> 2 tablespoons soy sauce

1. Preheat oven to 325°. Butter a large flameproof baking dish and set it aside.

2. Trim excess fat from tenderloins. Cut in ¾-inch medallions.

3. Season the medallions with salt and pepper.

4. In a heavy skillet melt the butter, add the olive oil, and heat until very hot. Add the medallions, a few at a time, and brown them on both sides. Remove browned medallions to buttered baking dish.

5. In the same skillet (add more butter and oil if necessary) sauté the garlic over medium heat. When translucent, add lemon rind, vermouth, mustard, and soy sauce. Simmer about 5 minutes, scraping the bottom of the pan well to deglaze. Pour sauce evenly over the medallions.

6. Cover the baking dish tightly with foil and place in the middle of the oven. Bake (braise) the medallions for 25 to 30 minutes.

❦

BARBECUED PORK TENDERLOIN

Cooking-out at Blueberry Hill (with 30 hungry guests waiting in the dining room) seemed a bit overwhelming, but with Tony's son, Chris, "on coals" as well as "mosquito patrol," the experience was fun and the results delicious. The barbecue sauce in this recipe acts as both a tenderizing marinade and flavorful sauce, and works equally well on chicken or grilled bluefish filets.

— *Arlyn Hertz*

SERVES 4 TO 6

> 2 pork tenderloins, each about 1 pound
> ½ cup peanut or vegetable oil
> ½ cup soy sauce
> ¼ cup honey
> ¼ cup molasses
> 1 teaspoon thyme
> 1 teaspoon paprika
> ½ teaspoon chili powder
> ¼ teaspoon curry powder
> 2 tablespoons vinegar

1. Prepare the sauce by mixing all of the ingredients (except the pork) in a medium saucepan. Place over medium heat and stir constantly until the sauce begins to bubble. Lower the heat and continue to cook the sauce, stirring occasionally, for another 5 minutes. Remove the pan from the heat, allow the sauce to cool, then transfer it to a tightly covered jar and refrigerate until you are ready to use it.

2. Prepare the meat for marinating at least 3 hours before serving time, preferably the morning of your cookout. Trim any excess fat from the tenderloins and slice them in medallions about ¾ inch thick.

3. Place the medallions in a glass baking dish large enough to hold the meat in one layer. Cover the meat with the barbecue sauce, cover the dish, then refrigerate until about 30 minutes before your coals are ready.

4. Start the coals. While they are getting hot, place the medallions on skewers. (If you use wooden skewers, soak them in water for 10 to 15 minutes before placing the meat on them. This prevents the wood from burning during the cooking process.)

5. Place the skewers on the hot, glowing coals. Turn frequently, basting the meat with the sauce each time you turn the skewers. Cooking time should be about 15 minutes, but this will depend on the temperature of your coals and the distance of the grill from the coals. It's best to test a piece after 10 minutes to check for doneness.

❦

HONEY-SMOKED PORK LOIN
WITH MUSTARD CREAM SAUCE

If you are unable to find smoked pork loin, regular pork loin will suffice— but it will not leave your kitchen smelling like a sweet summer cook-out on a frosty January night. — *Adria Lagasse*

SERVES 4

> 16 ounces honey-smoked boneless pork loin, cut into 1-inch slices
>
> 2 tablespoons olive oil
>
> 1 pint heavy cream
>
> 3 tablespoons honey mustard (use about 5 tablespoons if cooking an unsmoked pork loin)
>
> 2 tablespoons whole-grain mustard
>
> Freshly grated black pepper to taste

1. Heat the olive oil over high heat in a large, heavy skillet. Add the smoked pork loin slices. Cook about 4 minutes on each side. (For a fresh pork loin, cooking time will be about 7 minutes on each side.) Remove the pork from the pan and keep warm while preparing the sauce.

2. In the same skillet, reduce the heavy cream to a sauce-like consistency by cooking over high heat. Whisk the sauce frequently to avoid boiling over. This should take about 5 minutes.

3. Add both mustards and freshly ground pepper to the sauce, whisking until incorporated.
4. Spoon the sauce over the pork and serve.

❦

ROAST FRESH HAM

This was the first meal that I prepared as cook at Blueberry Hill. It was the weekend of Middlebury College graduation, and the inn was packed. The ham takes no time at all to prepare. Please accompany the ham with steamed raisin pudding (see the recipe on page 126)—it's a perfect match. — *Tory Sneff*

SERVES 10, PLUS LEFTOVERS

> 1 12-pound fresh ham
> Salt and freshly ground black pepper
> 2 cups dry white wine
> ½ cup olive oil
> 6 bay leaves
> 3 cloves
> 3 peppercorns

1. Peel the skin from the ham and trim the fat, leaving about a ¼-inch layer to protect the meat. Rub the meat well with salt and pepper.
2. Place the fresh ham in a large glass pan. Mix together the wine, olive oil, bay leaves, cloves, and peppercorns and pour over the meat. Marinate for 24 hours, turning frequently.
3. Preheat the oven to 350°.
4. Transfer the ham with its marinade to a roasting pan and roast for approximately 20 minutes per pound, basting frequently with the marinade.
5. Transfer the ham to a large platter and keep it hot. Strain the pan juices. Skim the fat from the pan juices and pour into a gravy bowl.
6. Slice the ham and serve it accompanied with steamed raisin pudding.

❧
PERFECT LAMB CHOPS

I prepared these lamb chops the evening that Paul Grimes, of the *New York Times,* and his wife, Mimi, joined us for the night. (His article, "In Search of the Perfect Vermont Inn," appeared on the front page of the travel section in July 1982.) The moistness of the chops is due to cooking them individually in foil packets. Prima! — *Tory Sneff*

SERVES 6

> 1 tablespoon finely chopped garlic
> ⅓ cup minced fresh mint and parsley (equal amounts of each, or to your taste)
> 4 tablespoons sweet butter
> 6 boned loin lamb chops, cut 1½ inches thick, about 6 ounces each
> 6 thin lemon slices
> 6 sprigs fresh mint
> 1 pound small mushroom caps, wiped clean
> Salt and freshly ground black pepper to taste

1. Preheat the oven to 350°.
2. Make a rough paste by mashing together the garlic, mint, parsley, and half the butter. Spread the herb butter on top of the lamb chops.
3. Arrange each chop on a piece of aluminum foil. Place a lemon slice and mint sprig on top of each chop. Spread the remaining butter over the mushroom caps and arrange them around the chops. Season with salt and pepper. Seal the foil packets and set them on a baking sheet.
4. Bake the chops 20 minutes for medium rare.
5. Transfer the packets to plates. Open the packets carefully, transfer the chops to plates, and pour the juices over the chops.

❧
CHICKEN CORDON BLEU

This was the first entrée I served at the inn after I'd "graduated" from waitress to assistant cook to cook. I wanted to mark my debut with something elegant and flavorful that could be prepared ahead of time, and this is what I came up with. The guests loved it, and it continues to be one of my favorite dishes for company. — *Elsie Sherrill*

SERVES 4

2 boneless, skinless chicken breasts, cut in half
4 slices Provolone cheese
4 slices prosciutto *or* Westphalian ham
⅔ cup plain bread crumbs
½ teaspoon *each* dried thyme, basil, and rosemary
2 eggs, lightly beaten
6 tablespoons sweet butter
2 shallots, minced
1 clove garlic, minced
½ pound mushrooms, washed, dried, and thinly sliced
1½ cups vermouth
1 cup heavy cream
¼ cup fresh parsley, chopped

1. Preheat the oven to 350°. Lightly butter a small baking dish.
2. Place each chicken breast between 2 sheets of waxed paper and pound out to ¼ inch thick.
3. Lay a slice of cheese, then a slice of prosciutto or ham on each breast, roll up jelly roll fashion, and secure with a toothpick.
4. Mix the bread crumbs with thyme, basil, and rosemary and place them in a large, flat dish.
5. Dip each rolled breast in the eggs, then roll in the breadcrumb mixture. Shake off any excess crumbs.
6. Melt 3 tablespoons of the butter in a large, heavy skillet over medium heat. When the butter is bubbling, add the breasts and brown evenly on all sides. This should take no longer than 3 minutes. Remove the breasts to the small baking dish. (You can prepare the chicken ahead up to this point, cover the dish, and refrigerate until you're ready to finish cooking the chicken.)
7. Remove the chicken from the refrigerator and let stand for 10 to 15 minutes. Bake, uncovered, for about 20 minutes.
8. While the chicken is baking prepare the sauce. Melt the remaining 3 tablespoons of butter in a medium saucepan over medium heat. Sauté the shallots and garlic for 1 minute, or until limp and translucent. Add the mushrooms and sauté for 5 minutes, stirring frequently.
9. When the liquid given off by the mushrooms has evaporated, add the vermouth and cook until it is reduced to ½ cup. Add the heavy cream, bring to a boil, then lower the heat and simmer about 10 minutes, or until thickened to desired consistency.
10. Serve the chicken (remember to remove the toothpicks!) with the sauce either spooned over or as an undersauce. Garnish with the fresh parsley.

♥

Stuffed Chicken Breasts Cooked in Champagne on a Bed of Shiitake Mushrooms

This is one of those wonderful recipes that has a glamorous ring to it but is easy to prepare. It is best with fresh shiitake mushrooms, but dried will do just fine. — *Irene C. Eilers*

SERVES 4

> 2 boneless, skinless chicken breasts, cut in half
> 8 ounces fresh shiitake mushrooms *or* 1 ounce dried
> 2½ cups champagne (medium-priced or better)
> 2 tablespoons sweet butter
> 2 tablespoons olive oil
> 2 tablespoons finely chopped shallots
> 1 teaspoon freshly grated ginger
> 1 tablespoon sweet butter
> 1 tablespoon olive oil
> 2 teaspoons finely chopped shallots
> 1 cup heavy cream
> Salt and freshly ground black pepper to taste, *or* use soy sauce in place of salt

1. Preheat the oven to 400°.
2. Place the breasts between wax paper and pound them thin, about ¼ inch. Set aside.
3. If using fresh shiitake mushrooms: remove the stems and thinly slice the caps. Cut the root off each stem and slice the stem into thick rounds. Place the 2 tablespoons each of butter and oil in a heavy skillet over medium-high heat. Add the 2 tablespoons of shallots and sauté lightly, then add the sliced mushrooms and sauté until the mushrooms just become limp. Sprinkle the grated ginger over the top.
4. For dried mushrooms: break the stems off the caps. Put both the stems and the caps into a bowl and cover with hot water. Soak until they are soft, at least several hours. Drain off the liquid and proceed as for fresh shiitakes.

5. Put several slices of the sautéed mushrooms in the center of each chicken breast, roll it up, and secure it with a toothpick. Heat the 1 tablespoon butter and 1 tablespoon olive oil in a heavy skillet. Add the breasts and lightly brown them on all sides. Remove the breasts from the pan, reserving the pan and the drippings.

6. Cover the bottom of a small baking dish with the remaining sautéed mushrooms, reserving the liquid. Place the browned breasts on top of the mushrooms and pour over 1½ cups of the champagne—enough to cover the mushrooms. Cover and bake in the preheated oven for 15 to 20 minutes.

7. While the breasts are baking, sauté the 2 teaspoons shallots in the pan drippings left from browning the chicken. Add the remaining cup of champagne and cook until it is reduced to half. Add the mushroom liquid from the other pan and the heavy cream and continue to reduce until the sauce thickens. Season the sauce with salt or soy sauce and pepper and set aside.

8. Remove the cooked breasts from the baking dish and remove the toothpicks. Set the breasts aside and keep warm. Remove the cooked mushrooms and some of the cooking liquid and add them to the reduction sauce. Cook over high heat until the sauce reaches the desired consistency. Adjust the seasoning and serve the breasts with a generous amount of the sauce.

❦

CHICKEN BREASTS STUFFED WITH SPINACH AND WATERCRESS

I stumbled across this combination one evening when I was short on spinach and determined to serve my characteristic "white and green" plate. It was a hit, and I have since discovered that this dish lends itself to endless variations on the theme. This particular version is delicious served with pasta tossed with olive oil, garlic, and fresh basil. — *Irene C. Eilers*

SERVES 4

> 2 boneless, skinless chicken breasts, each cut in half
> 1 leek
> 1 tablespoon olive oil
> ½ cup dry white wine
> 8 ounces fresh spinach
> 8 ounces watercress

3 ounces cream cheese (or a mild Chèvre) at room temperature
3 ounces Brie, at room temperature
Salt and freshly ground black pepper to taste
¼ teaspoon freshly ground nutmeg
1 tablespoon olive oil
1 tablespoon sweet butter
½ cup heavy cream

1. Preheat the oven to 400°.
2. Pound the breasts between waxed paper to an even thickness (about ¼ inch) and size. Set them aside.
3. Carefully wash the leek and remove the green top and root end. Slice the white part into rounds and wash again. (Leeks are sneaky grit retainers.) In a medium skillet, sauté the leek in 1 tablespoon olive oil. Add the wine, cover, and allow to steam until the leek is very soft. Add more wine if necessary. Drain the leek and set it aside.
4. Wash the spinach and watercress and remove the tough stems. Chop the leaves coarsely, then steam the leaves until they are barely wilted and retain their bright green color, about 1 to 2 minutes. Drain off all the liquid and set aside.
5. In a small bowl, mash together the Brie and cream cheese with a fork. Set it aside.
6. In a food processor fitted with a steel blade, purée the drained leek and 1 cup of the watercress-spinach mixture. Season with salt, pepper, and nutmeg.
7. Spread each chicken breast with 1 tablespoon of the cheese mixture and in the center put a line of the puréed greens. Roll up the breast and secure with a toothpick.
8. Heat the 1 tablespoon butter and 1 tablespoon olive oil over medium heat in a heavy skillet. Lightly brown the breasts on all sides. Put them in a small baking dish, cover, and bake in the preheated oven for 15 to 20 minutes.
9. While the chicken is baking, prepare the sauce. In a food processor fitted with a steel blade, purée the remaining watercress-spinach mixture. Place the purée in a saucepan and add the heavy cream. Cook over low heat for about 7 minutes, then add the remaining cheese mixture. Heat just long enough to melt the cheese but not to harm the color of the greens. Adjust the seasoning with additional freshly grated nutmeg.
10. Remove the toothpicks from the cooked breasts. Ladle a generous helping of the warm sauce on a plate and place a chicken breast on top of the sauce. (Or, if you prefer, pour the sauce *over* the chicken.) Serve immediately while the chicken and sauce are both piping hot.

CHICKEN IN BLUEBERRY SAUCE

Blueberry Hill didn't get its name out of thin air. By late August I was still knee deep in blueberries, and thus in self-defense started making batches of blueberry vinegar and blueberry jam. This recipe was inspired by the need to find a creative use for the vinegar and jam. I'm sure it would be equally as good using other homemade fruit jams, such as raspberry or peach.

— *Arlyn Hertz*

SERVES 4

2 whole boneless chicken breasts, skin on, cut in half

½ cup Blueberry Champagne Vinegar (see recipe on page 152)

¼ cup dry vermouth

1 teaspoon dried thyme

½ teaspoon dried marjoram

Salt and freshly ground black pepper to taste

½ cup honey-sweetened blueberry jam

1 teaspoon Dijon mustard

1 tablespoon sweet butter

4 fresh blueberry sprigs for garnish

1. Combine the chicken breast with the vinegar, vermouth, thyme, and marjoram in a bowl and marinate in the refrigerator for 4 hours, turning occasionally.

2. Preheat the oven to 350°.

3. Remove the chicken from the marinade and place the breasts in a glass baking dish. Season them with salt and pepper to taste. Reserve the marinade.

4. In a small saucepan over medium heat, heat the jam, mustard, butter, and 3 tablespoons of the reserved marinade. Bring to a gentle boil and then simmer for 5 minutes, stirring frequently.

5. Brush the chicken breasts with half of the blueberry sauce. Bake the chicken, uncovered, on the center rack of the oven for about 30 minutes. Continue to baste the chicken with the other half of the sauce. Before serving, place the chicken under the broiler for 3 minutes to crisp it.

6. Serve the chicken garnished with fresh blueberry sprigs.

PESTO-STUFFED CHICKEN BREASTS WITH MORNAY SAUCE

This chicken entrée is well worth the time and effort involved. You can simplify the process by preparing the pesto sauce and stuffing the chicken in advance, leaving the preparation of the Mornay sauce until serving time.

— Laurie Taylor

SERVES 4

Pan Sauce for Roasting Chicken
1 tablespoon sweet butter
1 shallot, minced
1 tablespoon fresh chives, minced
¼ cup white wine

Pesto Sauce
1 cup fresh basil, stemmed, washed, and patted dry
2 large cloves garlic
½ cup pine nuts
½ cup olive oil
½ cup freshly grated Parmesan cheese
½ cup freshly grated Romano cheese
Salt and freshly ground black pepper to taste

Chicken
2 whole boneless, skinless chicken breasts, cut in half
1 tablespoon olive oil

Mornay Sauce
3 tablespoons sweet butter
3 tablespoons unbleached white flour
2 cups milk
¼ teaspoon white pepper
2 tablespoons sweet butter at room temperature
1 cup freshly grated Parmesan cheese
4 sprigs fresh basil leaves for garnish

1. Preheat the oven to 350°.

2. Melt 1 tablespoon butter in a saucepan over low heat. Add the shallots, chives, and white wine. Cook until shallots are soft. Pour in an ovenproof shallow baking dish and set aside.

FOR THE PESTO SAUCE

3. Combine the basil, garlic and nuts in the bowl of a food processor fitted with a steel blade. Process for 15 seconds. With the motor running, add the olive oil. Shut the motor off and add the cheeses, salt, and pepper. Process briefly. Scrape out into a separate bowl and cover until ready to use.

4. Flatten the chicken breasts with the palms of your hand to tenderize. Spread each breast with ¼ cup of the pesto sauce. Roll breasts lengthwise like a jelly roll and secure each with a toothpick.

5. Heat 1 tablespoon olive oil in a sauté pan over high heat. Brown the chicken breasts on all sides, about 1 minute. Place breasts in the baking dish with the shallot mixture. Cover tightly with foil and bake for 30 minutes.

FOR THE MORNAY SAUCE

6. Melt 3 tablespoons butter in a heavy saucepan. Sprinkle in the flour and cook gently for about 5 minutes, stirring constantly. Let the mixture bubble but not brown. Remove the roux from the heat.

7. In a separate pan, bring the milk to a boil; remove from the heat. Add the boiling milk to the roux, whisking vigorously as boiling continues. When the bubbling ceases, return the pan to medium heat and bring the sauce back to a gentle boil. Cook 5 minutes, stirring constantly.

8. When sauce thickens to desired consistency, season with white pepper, softened butter, and Parmesan. Stir gently until butter and Parmesan are melted. Remove the sauce from the heat and cover to keep warm while the chicken is baking.

9. When chicken is baked, remove from the oven and remove the toothpicks. Slice each breast into ¼-inch pinwheels. Ladle ¼ to ½ cup of the warm Mornay sauce on each plate and arrange pinwheels of chicken on top. Garnish with a sprig of fresh basil.

❧
CHICKEN SERENI

The herbs in this recipe give the chicken an Italian flair. It's a great company dish, as all the preparation is done ahead of time, and it smells great when it's baking—but not as delicious as it tastes! — *Arlyn Hertz*

SERVES 8

> 4 whole chicken breasts, boned and skinned, cut in half and pounded until about ¼ inch thick
> 4 tablespoons sweet butter, at room temperature
> 1 teaspoon dried oregano
> 1 tablespoon freshly minced parsley
> 2 cloves garlic, minced fine
> ¾ cup plain bread crumbs
> ¾ cup grated Parmesan cheese
> ¼ teaspoon salt
> ⅛ teaspoon freshly ground black pepper
> ½ pound Monterey Jack or Mozzarella cheese, cut into 8 1½-inch-by-½-inch strips
> 5 tablespoons melted sweet butter
> Sprigs of fresh parsley for garnish

1. Make the herb butter: combine with a fork the 4 tablespoons of butter, oregano, parsley, and garlic. Set aside.
2. In a flat dish, stir together the bread crumbs, Parmesan cheese, salt, and pepper.
3. Spread the herb-butter mixture evenly over each breast. Place 1 cheese strip on each breast and roll up around the cheese. Secure with a toothpick.
4. Dip each rolled breast into the melted butter and then roll each breast in the breadcrumb mixture. Place the breasts seam-side down in an ungreased glass baking dish. Cover and refrigerate 4 hours (or overnight).
5. Remove chicken from the refrigerator at least ½ hour before baking.
6. Preheat the oven to 400°.
7. Bake the chicken uncovered for 25 minutes, or until the juices no longer run pink when the chicken is pierced with a fork. Remove the toothpicks.
8. Serve garnished with sprigs of fresh parsley.

MARINATED CHICKEN BREASTS WITH SWEET RED PEPPER PURÉE

The marinade in this recipe is quite versatile and can be used successfully on any meat or poultry. — *Lynn Levy*

SERVES 8

8 boneless, skinless chicken breast halves
8 fresh basil leaves, for garnish

Marinade
¾ cup vegetable oil
3 tablespoons fresh lemon juice
½ teaspoon salt
Freshly ground black pepper
3 tablespoons balsamic vinegar
6 tablespoons Dijon-style mustard
6 garlic cloves, minced
¼ cup chopped fresh basil

Pepper Purée
2 large sweet red peppers
¼ cup heavy cream
Salt and freshly ground black pepper to taste

1. Prepare marinade by mixing all the listed ingredients together.
2. Place the chicken breasts in a glass baking dish. Pour the marinade over the breasts, cover, and refrigerate at least 4 hours. Spoon the marinade over the breasts 2 to 3 times during this period. About one hour before cooking time, remove the baking dish from the refrigerator and bring it to room temperature.
3. Preheat the oven to 350°. Bake the chicken, uncovered, in the marinade for about 30 minutes.
4. While the chicken is baking prepare the sauce. Core and seed the red peppers and cut in large dice. Steam them 10 minutes or until tender.
5. Drain the peppers and purée them in a food processor fitted with a steel blade.

6. Place the purée in a heavy saucepan over medium heat. Bring to a low simmer and add the heavy cream. Add salt and pepper to taste.
7. To serve, spoon the hot purée over each chicken breast and garnish with a fresh basil leaf.

❦

CHICKEN BREASTS IN MUSTARD CREAM SAUCE

I think this was my favorite chicken recipe, and a favorite of the guests also. It's simple to prepare, yet elegant enough to serve as a main course at a Blueberry Hill wedding. — *Arlyn Hertz*

SERVES 4

> 2 whole boneless, skinless chicken breasts, cut in half
> Salt and freshly ground black pepper to taste
> 2 tablespoons sweet butter
> ½ cup white wine
> 3 scallions, minced
> ⅓ cup Dijon mustard
> ½ cup crème fraîche
> 1 scallion, minced, for garnish

1. Preheat oven to 350°. Butter a large, flameproof baking dish.
2. Season the breasts with salt and pepper.
3. Melt the butter in a heavy skillet over high heat. Cook the breasts about 1 minute on each side. Remove browned breasts to buttered baking dish. Add 3 tablespoons of the white wine, cover tightly with foil, and bake in a preheated oven for about 30 minutes.
4. While the breasts are baking, add the scallions to the skillet and cook over low heat until wilted. (Add more butter if necessary.)
5. Add the remaining wine to the skillet, raise the heat, and simmer for 5 minutes. Whisk in the mustard and simmer another 5 minutes.
6. Five minutes before the breasts are done, whisk in the crème fraîche and bring it to a boil. Boil for 2 minutes.
7. Remove the cooked breasts from the oven and put them on individual plates. Spoon the sauce over them and garnish with the minced scallions.

Soufflé Roll
with Chicken Béchamel Filling
and Roasted Red-Pepper Coulis

This soufflé roll is substantial enough to serve as a main course at dinner, or, thinly sliced, as a first course or light luncheon. The two sauces and the chicken can be prepared a day or two ahead of time and reheated at the time of assembly. — *Frances McDermott*

SERVES 8 (AS A MAIN COURSE)

Soufflé Roll
2½ cups milk
¼ pound sweet butter
1 cup flour
10 egg yolks
1 teaspoon salt
¼ teaspoon pepper
⅛ teaspoon cayenne pepper
10 egg whites

Béchamel Sauce
3 cups milk
6 tablespoons sweet butter
6 tablespoons flour
Salt and white pepper to taste

Chicken Filling
5 whole boneless chicken breasts
3 sweet red peppers, seeded and finely diced
4 scallions, finely diced

Red Pepper Coulis
10 sweet red peppers
4 cloves garlic, minced
¼ cup olive oil

FOR THE SOUFFLÉ ROLL

1. Preheat the oven to 325°. Grease a 15-by-10½-by-1-inch jelly-roll pan. Line it with waxed paper and thoroughly grease the paper.

2. Scald the milk and set aside. In another saucepan, melt the butter. Turn the heat off and add the flour. Return to low heat and cook 2 to 3 minutes. Turn off the heat again and whisk in the hot milk. Return to medium heat and bring the mixture to a boil, reduce to a simmer and stir until thick. Remove from the heat and add the egg yolks one at a time, beating well after each addition. Season the mixture with salt, pepper, and cayenne.

3. Beat the egg whites until stiff but not dry. Fold one-third of the whites into the mixture to lighten it. Fold remaining two-thirds of the whites gently, but thoroughly, into the mixture. Immediately turn the mixture into the jelly-roll pan and bake about 25 minutes. As soon as you remove it from the oven, invert the soufflé roll onto a dish towel covered with waxed paper. Peel off the waxed paper from the bottom of the roll. Roll up the soufflé the long way in the towel and paper. Let cool.

FOR THE BÉCHAMEL SAUCE

4. Scald the milk. In a separate saucepan, melt the butter over low heat. Remove from the heat and add the flour, return to the heat and cook over low heat for 2 to 3 minutes. Remove from the heat, and whisk in the scalded milk. Return to the heat and bring to a boil, stirring constantly. Continue to simmer and stir over medium heat until thickened. Season to taste.

FOR THE FILLING

5. Preheat the oven to 325°. Line a sheet pan with waxed paper or parchment. Dry-poach the breasts: place them on the prepared pan and cover with another sheet of waxed paper or parchment. Bake for 10 to 15 minutes. Breasts should be firm to the touch and when pierced the juices should run clear. Let cool and chop fine.

6. Mix together the chopped chicken, diced peppers, and scallions and stir them into the Béchamel sauce. Set aside.

FOR THE RED PEPPER COULIS

7. Roast the red peppers: place them on a baking sheet in a 500° oven for about 30 minutes, or until the skins are blistered and charred.

8. Place the charred peppers in a paper bag or large plastic container for about 20 minutes, until completely cool. Place them under cold running water and remove the skin, seeds, and tops.

9. In a food processor fitted with a steel blade, purée the peppers and the garlic. Slowly add the olive oil. Transfer the purée to a saucepan and heat slowly to warm the sauce.

10. Preheat the oven to 350°. Lightly butter a large baking pan.
11. Unroll the soufflé and spread the chicken-Béchamel filling evenly over it. Roll back up lengthwise, without the towel and waxed paper. Carefully set the roll, seam side down, in the prepared baking pan. Cover the pan loosely with aluminum foil and bake for 15 to 20 minutes.
12. To serve, cut into ¾-inch slices for a first course or 1½-inch slices for a main course. Spoon the heated Red Pepper Coulis over the slices.

❦

CORNISH HENS BROIL-ROASTED IN WINE

Removing the backbone from the hens takes practice, but once I learned the technique, this quickly became my favorite entrée. — *Tory Sneff*

SERVES 6

> 3 Cornish game hens
> Salt and freshly ground black pepper to taste
> ½ teaspoon dried tarragon
> ½ cup olive oil
> 1 medium onion, minced
> 3 tablespoons sweet butter
> 1 cup grated Swiss cheese
> Dry white wine

1. Cut the hens in half and remove the backbone: Using a sharp, narrow knife (preferably a boning knife) slip the tip of the blade between one end of the backbone and the skin. Work your way along the bone, separating it from the skin and ribs. Cut at each end as necessary to release the backbone from the bird. To form a neat package, make a small slit on each side of breastbone tip and tuck drumstick ends into the skin slits.
2. Season both sides of the hens with salt, pepper, and tarragon. Sprinkle the breasts with the olive oil and minced onion.
3. Marinate the hens for a few hours in the refrigerator.
4. Preheat the oven to 400°.
5. Scrape off the marinade and dry the hens. Arrange hens, skin-side down, in a broiler pan. Dot with butter and brown under the broiler for 5 minutes. Flip and brown on the other side.

6. Place the hens skin-side up in a large baking dish and strew grated cheese over them. Pour enough white wine into the pan to form ¼ inch of liquid. Place the pan in the preheated oven for 30 to 40 minutes, basting every 10 minutes. Birds are done when juices run clear yellow when pierced with a fork in the thigh.

❦

DUCK GLAZED WITH CURRY AND HONEY

Duck is easy to cook, very rich yet not expensive. The addition of curry and honey is a nice change from the more traditional duck à l'orange.

— *Tory Sneff*

SERVES 8

2 whole ducks
3 tablespoons curry powder
2 garlic cloves, minced
1 teaspoon turmeric
½ teaspoon Tabasco sauce, or other hot pepper sauce
½ cup honey
¼ cup freshly squeezed orange juice
¼ cup freshly squeezed lemon juice

1. Preheat the oven to 350°.
2. Rub the ducks inside and out with 1½ tablespoons of the curry powder mixed with the garlic, turmeric, and Tabasco.
3. In a small bowl, mix together the honey, orange juice, lemon juice, and remaining curry powder. Set aside.
4. Place the ducks on a rack in a large roasting pan and roast for 1½ hours.
5. During the last half hour of roasting, baste often with the honey–orange juice mixture. Raise the oven temperature to 475° during the last 15 minutes of roasting to crisp the skin.
6. Quarter the ducks to serve.

Duck Breasts
with Black Currant Sauce

The beauty of cooking in Vermont in the summer is the availability of fresh produce and fresh, local meats. One of my favorite meals used fresh duck and wild currants. Fresh currants, which grew readily in Blueberry Hill's backyard, are much tarter than the dried variety. You may want to adjust the sweetness of the sauce by adding more liqueur when using fresh currants.

— Adria Lagasse

SERVES 4

4 boneless duck breasts
1 quart veal or beef stock
½ to ¾ cup Framboise liqueur
2 to 4 tablespoons Cointreau or Grand Marnier
6 tablespoons butter
½ cup fresh or dried currants

1. Preheat the oven to 450°.
2. Using a sharp knife, make 2 lengthwise and 2 crosswise slits in the skin of each duck breast.
3. Place each breast, skin-side down, in a very hot, unoiled skillet. Cook until the skin has turned a deep golden brown, about 3 to 5 minutes.
4. Place each breast, skin-side up, in a small baking pan and place in the oven. Cook until desired doneness. (Medium rare should take about 10 minutes.)
5. Prepare the sauce while the breasts are in the oven. In a large, heavy saucepan, cook the stock over high heat. Boil until the stock has reduced by half.
6. When the stock has reduced to about 2 cups, add the liqueurs and continue to cook for 5 minutes.
7. Lower the heat and whisk in the butter, one tablespoon at a time. Add the currants and remove from the heat.
8. Remove the duck breasts from the oven and let them rest for 5 minutes. Slice each breast crosswise into 6 to 8 pieces and fan onto a plate.
9. Spoon the sauce over each breast and serve immediately.

❦
TRUITE À L'ANTOINE
(TONY'S TROUT)

Catching trout out of your favorite pond is made particularly easy at Blue-berry Hill, where the pond is stocked. They bite best early in the morning, so consider serving this entrée to special breakfast guests as well as at lunch or dinner. — *Tony Clark*

SERVES 4

> 4 6- to 8-inch rainbow trout (if smaller, serve 2 per person),
> cleaned and heads removed
> 1 cup unbleached white flour
> ¼ teaspoon salt
> ¼ teaspoon freshly ground white pepper
> 6 tablespoons sweet butter
> 1 clove garlic, minced fine
> Juice of 1 lemon
> ½ cup fresh dill, chopped fine
> 1 cup toasted slivered almonds

1. Rinse the trout under cold water and pat them dry.
2. In a large flat dish, mix the flour with the salt and pepper. Lightly coat each trout with the seasoned flour.
3. Heat the butter in a large, heavy skillet over medium heat (being careful not to burn it) until bubbly, but not smoking. Add the garlic and sauté 30 seconds.
4. Add the trout and sauté for about 4 minutes. Turn and sauté 3 minutes on the other side. Remove the trout to a warm platter.
5. Add the chopped dill and the lemon juice to the skillet and sauté about 30 seconds, deglazing the pan.
6. Serve the trout with the lemon-dill butter. Garnish each serving with ¼ cup of the almonds—and wish you hadn't let that big one get away!

❦
FRESH RAINBOW TROUT
WITH DILLED HOLLANDAISE

Trout season in Vermont begins in May, and a special memory is serving trout for dinner caught that afternoon in the pond behind Blueberry Hill. This dish is equally good with fish purchased at your local fish market, or, if you're lucky, caught at *your* local fishing hole. — *Laurie Taylor*

SERVES 4

> 3 eggs yolks
> 1½ tablespoons fresh lemon juice
> Pinch of cayenne pepper
> 1 cup sweet butter, melted and heated till bubbly
> Salt and freshly ground white pepper to taste
> 2 tablespoons finely chopped fresh dill
> ½ cup unbleached white flour
> 1 tablespoon fresh thyme leaves
> Salt and freshly ground black pepper to taste
> 4 whole rainbow trout (about 6 ounces each), cleaned and heads removed. Extend the belly cavity so that the fish can be opened and laid flat, "butterfly" fashion.
> 4 tablespoons sweet butter
> 4 sprigs fresh dill for garnish

1. Process the egg yolks, lemon juice, and cayenne in a blender for 30 seconds.

2. With the blender running, pour in the hot butter in a slow, thin stream so that the resulting sauce is thick and creamy. Add the salt and freshly ground white pepper and the fresh dill and blend until just combined.

3. Transfer the sauce to the top of a double boiler over hot water. Cover and keep warm while cooking the trout.

4. Mix the flour, thyme, salt, and pepper in a shallow dish. Dip each trout in the flour mixture, lightly coating the entire fish.

5. Melt the 4 tablespoons butter in a large, heavy skillet over medium-high heat. Place the trout in the skillet, flesh-side down. Cook for 5 minutes. Flip the fish and cook another 2 minutes to crisp the skin.

6. Serve on warm plates, placing the trout flesh-side up. Ladle ¼ cup of the warm dill Hollandaise sauce across the fish and garnish with fresh dill.

❦
STUFFED FILET OF SOLE

This is another great company dish, as you can prepare the fish ahead of time and then bake it at the last minute. — *Laurie Caswell*

SERVES 6

1½ cups coarse bread crumbs
½ teaspoon oregano
½ teaspoon leaf thyme
½ teaspoon salt
½ teaspoon basil
1 teaspoon dill
¼ pound fresh oysters or cleaned salad shrimp, chopped
¼ cup chopped scallions
1 teaspoon sweet butter
2 cloves garlic, finely chopped
3 tablespoons dry white wine
6 medium (5 ounce) sole filets
½ cup sweet butter
½ cup dry white wine
Salt and freshly ground black pepper to taste
Lemon wedges and fresh dill sprigs for garnish

1. Preheat the oven to 350°. Lightly butter a large glass baking dish.
2. In a medium bowl, mix the bread crumbs with the oregano, thyme, salt, basil, and dill. Mix in the oysters or shrimp.
3. In a small skillet, sauté the scallions and garlic in 1 teaspoon butter until limp and translucent. Add this to the breadcrumb mixture. Moisten with 3 tablespoons dry white wine, or enough to bind stuffing together.
4. Place 2 tablespoons of the stuffing on one end of each filet. Roll the filets and fasten with toothpicks. Place in prepared baking dish.
5. In a small saucepan, melt ½ cup butter, then add ½ cup wine. Pour this over the fish. Sprinkle with salt, freshly ground black pepper, and some additional dill.
6. Bake for about 12 to 15 minutes, being careful not to overcook.
7. Serve with lemon wedges and fresh sprigs of dill.

Tilefish with Lime Beurre Blanc

Tilefish is a mild white fish, as delicate in flavor and consistency as sole. Even though you buy it fileted, check carefully for the many tiny bones that are characteristic of this fish. — *Frances McDermott*

SERVES 4

> 4 tilefish filets, each about 6 ounces
> ¼ cup dry white wine
> Juice of one lemon
> 4 tablespoons sweet butter
> ⅛ teaspoon salt
> ⅛ teaspoon ground white pepper
> ⅓ cup freshly squeezed lime juice
> ⅓ cup dry white wine
> ⅓ cup finely chopped shallots
> ½ teaspoon salt
> ¼ teaspoon ground white pepper
> 6 tablespoons sweet butter
> 1 fresh lime, thinly sliced for garnish

1. Preheat the oven to 350°. Lightly grease a 13½-by-8¾-inch glass baking dish.
2. Place the filets in a single layer in the baking dish. Pour the ¼ cup white wine and juice of one lemon evenly over the fish. Dot each filet with one tablespoon of butter, then lightly season with ⅛ teaspoon each of salt and pepper.
3. Cover the dish tightly with foil and bake for about 15 minutes.
4. While the fish is baking, prepare the beurre blanc: place lime juice, ⅓ cup wine, shallots, ½ teaspoon salt, and ¼ teaspoon pepper in a heavy nonreactive saucepan. Cook over medium heat until the liquid is reduced to about 3 tablespoons. Lower the heat and whisk in the 6 tablespoons of butter, 1 tablespoon at a time.
5. Strain the sauce and serve over the fish. Garnish each filet with a slice of lime.

❦
SWORDFISH STEAKS
WITH DIJON TARRAGON SAUCE

The meaty flavor of swordfish stands up to this rich classic sauce. Fresh tarragon is preferable, but substitute dry tarragon (half the amount indicated for fresh) if you absolutely can't find fresh herbs. By the way, this sauce also goes well with beef tenderloin. — *Laurie Taylor*

SERVES 4

4 swordfish steaks, about ½ pound each, cut 1 inch thick
1 cup dry white wine or vermouth
Salt and freshly ground black pepper to taste
1 tablespoon chopped fresh tarragon
1 tablespoon chopped fresh basil
1 tablespoon minced shallots
½ cup dry white wine or vermouth
2 tablespoons tarragon vinegar
2 tablespoons chopped fresh tarragon
Freshly ground black pepper, one good grinding
1 cup heavy cream
¼ cup dairy sour cream
½ cup Dijon mustard
Salt to taste

1. Preheat the oven to 375°.
2. Place the swordfish steaks in a single layer in a glass baking dish. Pour 1 cup of wine or vermouth around the fish and sprinkle with 1 tablespoon each of tarragon and basil. Add salt and pepper to taste. Set aside while preparing the sauce.
3. In a heavy saucepan, combine ½ cup wine or vermouth, vinegar, 2 tablespoons tarragon, and the pepper.
4. Place the pan over medium-high heat and cook until the liquid is reduced by half.
5. Mix together the heavy cream, sour cream, and mustard, and whisk the mixture into the wine reduction. Simmer uncovered over low heat, stirring occasionally until it reaches the desired consistency. Season with salt and pepper as needed. Cover and keep warm until the fish is baked.

---

6. Bake the fish on the middle rack of the oven for 10 minutes. Test for doneness with a fork and bake, if necessary, for 2 minutes longer. Test again.

7. Using a slotted spatula, transfer the cooked fish to warm plates and place 2 tablespoons of the warm Dijon tarragon sauce in the center of each steak. Serve immediately.

❦

Fresh Salmon
in Ginger-Lime-Sambuca Sauce

The Sambuca adds a unique and subtle flavor to this sauce without over-powering the delicate flavor of the salmon. — *Arlyn Hertz*

SERVES 8

> 8 fresh salmon steaks, cut 1 inch thick
> 1-inch piece of fresh ginger, peeled
> 1 teaspoon grated lime zest
> ½ cup sweet butter, at room temperature
> ¼ teaspoon salt
> 4 tablespoons freshly squeezed lime juice
> ¼ cup Sambuca
> 8 slices lime for garnish

1. Preheat the broiler and lightly grease the broiler pan.

2. Wipe the salmon with a damp cloth and place the steaks in a single layer on the broiler pan.

3. In a food processor fitted with a steel blade, blend until smooth the ginger, lime zest, butter, salt, and 2 tablespoons of lime juice. Set aside.

4. In a small saucepan, cook the remaining 2 tablespoons of lime juice with the Sambuca over moderate heat for about 5 minutes. Add the ginger-butter mixture, a little at a time. Cook for 5 minutes over low heat.

5. Brush the salmon steaks with sauce. Broil about 4 inches from the heat for 5 minutes. Turn the steaks, brush with more sauce, and broil for another 5 minutes, or until the salmon flakes easily when prodded in the thickest portion with a fork. Serve garnished with the fresh lime slices.

🍎
BROILED SALMON
TOPPED WITH SAUTÉED SCALLOPS

This is a simple summer meal, yet very elegant. — *Tory Sneff*
(If you ever visit the inn, ask Tony about the Goshen fellows who stole and buried a truck full of scallops—a great story, but too lengthy to repeat here.)

SERVES 6

Salmon

  1 cup sauternes
  ½ cup salad oil
  2 tablespoons wine vinegar
  2 teaspoons soy sauce
  2 tablespoons chopped scallions
  6 salmon steaks, cut ½ inch thick

Sautéed Scallops

  Flour
  1½ pounds bay scallops, well dried
  6 tablespoons unsalted butter
  3 tablespoons chopped fresh parsley
  1 teaspoon each chopped fresh tarragon and chives
  Salt and freshly ground pepper
  Lemon wedges and green grape clusters for garnish

FOR THE SALMON

nes, olive oil, soy sauce, and scallions and pour over the
a large, shallow glass dish. Marinate the steaks in the
:veral hours or overnight, turning occasionally.

salmon from the marinade and place on a broiler
ies from the heat source about 5 minutes on each side,
isly several times with the marinade.

SCALLOPS

1 is broiling, lightly flour the scallops. Heat the butter
intil foaming. Add the scallops and sauté very quickly,
he pan until lightly browned and cooked through. Bay
only 2 to 3 minutes.

4. Sprinkle with parsley, tarragon, chives, salt, and pepper.
5. To serve, put the salmon steaks on hot plates and place the scallops between the "legs." Garnish with lemon slices and grape clusters.

❦

SCALLOPS GERALDINE

Serve this dish either in large scallop shells surrounded by buttered green noodles, or directly on any hot pasta. This recipe is equally good prepared with fresh shrimp. — *Arlyn Hertz*

SERVES 4

¼ cup sweet butter
1 pound fresh sea scallops
Salt and freshly ground black pepper to taste
2 tablespoons minced shallots
2 tablespoons warm cognac
¼ cup tomato paste
½ cup plus 1 tablespoon heavy cream or crème fraîche
1 tablespoon minced fresh basil
1 tablespoon minced fresh chives
1 egg yolk, lightly beaten
¼ cup chopped fresh parsley

1. In a large skillet, melt the butter over medium heat. Add the scallops, sprinkle with salt and pepper, and cook about 5 minutes or until the scallops are cooked through. (Do not overcook!) Remove to a warm platter.
2. Add the shallots to the skillet and cook 1 minute. Next add the warm cognac and carefully ignite. When the flame goes out, add the tomato paste and cook 1 minute over high heat.
3. Stir in ½ cup of the cream or crème fraîche, the basil, and chives. Lower the heat and cook about 30 seconds.
4. Beat the egg yolk lightly with the remaining tablespoon of cream and add to the sauce. Raise the heat, add the warm scallops and stir constantly until the scallops are very hot, but *do not let the sauce boil*. Serve immediately, garnished with freshly chopped parsley.

GRILLED BOURBON SHRIMP KEBABS

This is great summertime fare, using fresh shrimp and fresh summer veggies.

— *Laurie Taylor*

SERVES 6

1 clove garlic, minced

½ cup olive oil

½ cup soy sauce

½ cup red wine vinegar

1 tablespoon tomato sauce or ketchup

1 tablespoon bourbon

1 tablespoon brown sugar

2 tablespoons chopped scallion greens

Freshly ground black pepper to taste

24 large whole shrimp, shelled, deveined, and
cut butterfly style

6 scallions, trimmed and cut to include 3 inches of greens, *or*
1 large Vidalia onion, cut in chunks

1 red pepper, seeded and cut in sixths

1 medium zucchini, cut in six thick slices

6 cherry tomatoes, washed and stemmed

6 artichoke hearts (preferably unmarinated), drained, halved
or left whole

1. Combine the garlic, oil, soy sauce, vinegar, tomato sauce or ketchup, bourbon, brown sugar, scallions, salt, and pepper in a medium-size bowl. Mix the marinade well.

2. Place the shrimp and cut-up vegetables in the bottom of a large shallow dish and cover with the marinade. Cover with plastic wrap and marinate in the refrigerator at least one hour, stirring occasionally.

3. Prepare the fire and let burn until the coals are medium-hot and glowing. If you use wooden skewers, soak them in water about 10 to 15 minutes before stringing on the shrimp and vegetables. This prevents the wood from burning as you cook the kebabs.

4. Remove the shrimp and vegetables from the refrigerator and make up kebabs by alternating vegetables and shrimp on skewers. (Skewer the scallion pieces in the center, not lengthwise.) Reserve some of the marinade for basting.

5. Grill the kebabs over the coals, turning and basting often until the vegetables are tender, about 10 minutes.

6. Serve on a bed of rice or lightly buttered linguine.

❦

LOBSTER AND CRAB RAVIOLI WITH ROASTED GARLIC CREAM SAUCE

This dish was prepared for a prenuptial dinner that I did for a couple who were married at Blueberry Hill. It went over so well that I used it on many evenings thereafter. At first glance the recipe appears rather time-consuming and complex, but if you prepare the ingredients in stages (make the pasta dough a day or more in advance), you will find it is really quite simple.

— *Adria Lagasse*

SERVES 6 TO 8

Pasta Dough (makes 1½ pounds)
1½ cups semolina flour (fine grind)

1½ cups all-purpose flour

2 teaspoons salt

4 eggs

2 tablespoons extra-virgin olive oil

Filling
2 pounds lobster meat, fresh or frozen

1 pound crab meat, fresh or frozen

2 eggs

2 medium sweet red peppers

1 cup bread crumbs

1½ cups ricotta cheese

1 cup Boursin cheese (see recipe page 43 if you wish to make your own herbed cheese)

Egg Wash
2 egg yolks diluted with

2 tablespoons water or milk

Sauce

  1 head of garlic, left intact (do not peel)
  Olive oil
  Salt
  1 quart heavy cream
  Salt and freshly ground black pepper to taste

PASTA DOUGH

1. Place the flours and salt in a food processor fitted with a steel blade. Pulse to blend.
2. With the motor running, add the eggs and the olive oil. Process until the dough begins to mass on the blade (about 1 to 2 minutes).
3. Remove the dough from the processor and knead on a floured surface until smooth (1 to 2 minutes).
4. Wrap the dough tightly in plastic and let it rest at least 2 hours in the refrigerator (you can prepare the dough a day or two ahead of time and refrigerate) before rolling and cutting into desired shape.

FILLING

1. Combine the lobster and crab meat in a large bowl. Be sure that the cartilage is removed from both.
2. Beat the eggs and add to the lobster-crab mixture.
3. Remove the seeds from the peppers and cut into fine dice. Add to the above mixture.
4. Add the remaining ingredients and mix well. The mixture should hold together well; if it is too wet, add more bread crumbs to bind.

EGG WASH

1. Prepare the egg wash when ready to roll and fill the pasta.

SAUCE

1. Preheat the oven to 350°.
2. Rub olive oil over the entire head of garlic and lightly salt.
3. Place the garlic in a small pan and roast in the oven for approximately 30 minutes. The skin should be lightly brown.
4. Remove the garlic from the oven and let cool.
5. Place the cream in a heavy saucepan and cook over high heat. Cook until cream is reduced to a saucelike consistency. Stir the cream frequently so it does not boil over. This should take no more than 10 minutes.

6. While the cream is reducing, separate the cloves of garlic from the head and squeeze the pulp into a food processor fitted with a steel blade. Take about ½ cup of the reduced cream, let it cool about 1 minute, and add it to the processor. Process until garlic is puréed. Return purée to the cream sauce.

7. Season the sauce with salt and pepper. If you're not ready to use it immediately, keep warm in a double boiler placed over low heat.

TO ASSEMBLE AND SERVE

1. Using either a hand crank or electric pasta machine, roll the pasta dough into thin, rectangular sheets about 10 inches by 15 inches. If you are unfamiliar with working with pasta dough, please refer to any Italian cookbook on basic pasta-making instructions.

2. Place heaping teaspoons of the crab-lobster mixture onto one sheet of the pasta. Space the mounds according to the size and shape of the raviolis you want.

3. Using a pastry brush, spread an even layer of egg wash around the edges of the pasta sheet and between the mounds of lobster-crab mixture.

4. Carefully place another sheet of pasta over the prepared sheet and press down around the edges and mounds of mixture to seal well.

5. Using either a rolling cutter with a serrated edge or a rounded cookie cutter, cut ravioli into desired shape and place on a well floured surface. Cover with a damp towel. Continue to prepare ravioli following the above procedure.

6. Bring a large pot of water to a boil. Pot should be large enough to cook ravioli without crowding. Add a dash of salt and wait until the water returns to a rapid boil. (If you find your pot is not large enough to accommodate all the ravioli without crowding, cook the ravioli in two batches, removing the first batch with a slotted spoon. Be sure the water has returned to a full boil before adding the second batch.)

7. Drop the ravioli into the rapidly boiling water and cook for 30 to 45 seconds. Drain.

8. To serve, spoon the desired amount of hot roasted garlic cream sauce over each serving of ravioli.

VEGETABLES
&
SIDE DISHES

Asparagus
with Lemon Crumbs

I am an asparagus aficionado. Asparagus dishes are so simple to prepare, yet they attract so much attention whenever they appear on the plate.
— *Tory Sneff*

SERVES 4

2 pounds asparagus, trimmed and cleaned
½ cup dry bread crumbs
½ cup sweet butter, melted
Grated rind of 2 lemons
Salt and freshly ground black pepper to taste
¼ cup sweet butter, browned

1. Steam the asparagus until bright green and tender. Drain it well and place it on a warm platter and keep it covered.
2. Sauté the bread crumbs gently in ½ cup melted butter for about 5 minutes, or until golden.
3. Add the grated lemon rind, salt, and pepper to taste. Scatter the mixture over the asparagus stalks and pour the browned butter over them. Serve immediately.

Asparagus Vinaigrette

Cold asparagus is a nice accompaniment to any meal. It's especially nice for company, as it can be prepared a day ahead of time. The longer it marinates the tastier it gets. — *Arlyn Hertz*

SERVES 6

2½ pounds of fresh asparagus, washed and trimmed
    of tough stems
3 tablespoons cider vinegar
¼ cup safflower oil
2 tablespoons olive oil
1 teaspoon salt
Dash of freshly ground white pepper
½ teaspoon sugar
1 hard boiled egg, chopped

1. Blanch the asparagus in boiling water for 1 minute, then immediately plunge into cold water. Drain completely.
2. Make the marinade by whisking together the vinegar, oils, salt, pepper, and sugar.
3. Arrange the asparagus in one layer in a *glass* baking dish. Pour the marinade over it.
4. Cover the dish tightly with plastic wrap and refrigerate for at least 4 hours, turning spears and spooning marinade over them several times.
5. To serve, bring asparagus to room temperature and garnish with the chopped hard-cooked egg.

❦

BRANDIED CARROTS

This recipe comes from Megan Sutton, who worked as manager of the Blueberry Hill ski shop. It's a family recipe that she got from her mother. Thanks, Megan. Thanks, Erica. — *Alan Levy*

SERVES 4

> 1 pound carrots, washed and peeled
> ½ cup sweet butter, melted
> 2 tablespoons sugar
> ½ teaspoon salt
> ⅓ cup brandy
> ¼ cup chopped fresh parsley for garnish

1. Preheat the oven to 350°.
2. Cut the carrots in julienne strips about 2 inches long and ¼ inch wide. Arrange in a baking dish just large enough to hold them comfortably.
3. Pour the melted butter over the carrots, then sprinkle them with the sugar and salt. Add the brandy.
4. Cover the dish tightly and bake for 1 hour. Serve garnished with the chopped parsley.

❦
Carrots with Coriander-Fennel Butter

This is an unusual, sweet and spicy way to prepare carrots.

— Frances McDermott

SERVES 4

> 1 pound carrots, peeled and sliced on the diagonal
> 4 tablespoons sweet butter
> ¼ cup Vermont maple syrup
> 2 teaspoons ground coriander
> 1 tablespoon fennel seed

1. Bring a large pot of water to a boil and blanch the carrots for about 3 minutes or until crisp-tender. Plunge into cold water and drain well.
2. In a heavy skillet, melt the butter over medium heat. Stir in the carrots and sauté for 1 minute. Add the maple syrup and continue to sauté until the liquid has reduced to glaze the carrots.
3. Remove carrots from the heat and add the herbs. Toss well.

❦
Baked Garlic

When you bake garlic in this fashion, it becomes a sweet and fragrant vegetable. It can also be served as an hors d'oeuvre or first course, with rounds of toasted French bread and warm goats' cheese sprinkled with fresh herbs.

— Frances McDermott

SERVES 4

> 2 large (elephant ear) whole bulbs of fresh garlic
> 1 to 2 cups chicken stock

1. Preheat the oven to 350°.
2. Trim the paperlike skin off the garlic cloves, being careful to leave the bulbs whole and intact. Next cut the top ¼ inch from the garlic so that the bulb can open when it has baked thoroughly.
3. Place the bulbs in a small pan or oven-proof dish. Add enough chicken stock to reach halfway up the garlic.
4. Bake for 45 minutes to 1 hour, or until the garlic bulbs are soft. Baste often to keep the bulbs moist, and add more stock as necessary.
5. To serve, cut bulbs in half and serve ½ bulb per person.

BRAISED LEEKS

Leeks, like lentils, are another childhood favorite of mine. Serving them at the inn was always a delight because many Americans at that time were not familiar with leeks as a vegetable. They're delicious served with fish or lamb.

— *Irene C. Eilers*

SERVES 4

> 6 medium leeks
> 1 tablespoon sweet butter
> 1 tablespoon olive oil
> ½ cup good quality white wine
> Pinch of sugar
> Salt to taste
> Freshly grated nutmeg to taste

1. Cut off the green tops and roots and wash the leeks thoroughly. Cut into thick slices and soak in water to remove any remaining dirt. Keep rinsing if necessary.
2. Melt the butter and olive oil in a heavy skillet and sauté the leeks until they begin to look milky but not browned. Add the wine, sugar, and salt and grate a generous amount of nutmeg over the top. Cover and simmer until tender, approximately 10 to 15 minutes. Add more wine (or water) if all the liquid evaporates before the leeks are done. Serve immediately.

POTATO AND TURNIP PURÉE

Now that I'm in the produce business, I realize how boring winter vegetables can be. Here is a way to spark up the old standbys. — *Laurie Taylor*

SERVES 4

> 2 medium all-purpose potatoes
> 1 small rutabaga turnip
> ½ teaspoon salt
> 3 tablespoons sweet butter
> 1 tablespoon Vermont maple syrup
> 1 tablespoon dry sherry
> Salt and freshly ground black pepper to taste

1. Peel the potatoes and the rutabaga and cut them into large chunks.
2. In a large saucepan, bring 4 cups of water to a boil. Add the salt, the potatoes, and the rutabaga and boil for about 30 minutes.
3. Drain the vegetables well and let them cool.
4. Place the potatoes, rutabaga, butter, syrup, and sherry in the bowl of a food processor fitted with a steel blade. Process until well mixed but not over-puréed.
5. Return the mixture to a heavy skillet and reheat over medium heat, stirring occasionally. Add the salt and pepper to taste. Note: The more you cook the purée the tastier it gets.

❦

SAUTEÉD SHIITAKE MUSHROOMS WITH BALSAMIC VINEGAR

I like to sauté vegetables because I feel it retains their flavor and texture best. At Blueberry Hill we have large cast-iron pans that provide additional dietary iron, allow me to sauté enough vegetables for a crowd—and give me a work-out when I have to carry them to the dishwasher. — *Frances McDermott*

SERVES 8

> 1 pound fresh shiitake mushrooms
> ¼ cup melted sweet butter
> ¼ cup olive oil
> ¼ cup balsamic vinegar
> Salt and freshly ground black pepper to taste

1. Rinse the mushrooms, pat dry, and slice.
2. In a large heavy skillet, heat the butter and olive oil over medium-high heat. Add the mushrooms and sauté until just cooked. Add the balsamic vinegar and continue to cook until the mushrooms are coated and the pan is deglazed. Season with salt and pepper and serve immediately.

SPINACH AND ARTICHOKE SOUFFLÉ

A tasty and rich vegetable side dish that makes a nice accompaniment to a roast or grilled chicken. — *Laurie Caswell*

SERVES 6

> 1 pound fresh spinach, washed, destemmed, and chopped
> 4 tablespoons sweet butter
> ½ cup chopped onion
> ½ cup chopped green pepper
> ½ cup grated Parmesan cheese
> 2 cups sour cream
> 1 16-ounce can artichoke hearts (in water), drained and diced fine
> Salt and freshly ground black pepper to taste

1. Preheat the oven to 350°. Lightly butter a medium-size soufflé or casserole dish.
2. Steam the spinach and drain well. Squeeze out as much liquid as possible. Set aside.
3. In a skillet over medium heat, sauté the onions and peppers in the butter for about 5 minutes or until the onions are translucent. Combine with the spinach, then add all the other ingredients.
4. Pour mixture into the prepared baking dish, sprinkle with some more grated cheese, and bake for 30 minutes or until hot and bubbly.

TOMATOES PROVENÇAL

The long, slow cooking of the tomatoes leaves me time to attend to the other details of the meal. Ripe tomatoes, another garden-fresh favorite of mine, accent the greens and browns usually on the plate. — *Tory Sneff*

SERVES 4 TO 6

> 1 cup *fresh*—not dry—white bread crumbs
> 2 cloves garlic, minced
> 3 tablespoons chopped fresh parsley
> 2 tablespoons olive oil
> Dash of salt

½ teaspoon freshly ground black pepper

½ teaspoon dry mustard

5 unpeeled ripe firm tomatoes (The skin helps the tomatoes keep their shape during the slow cooking.)

3 tablespoons olive oil

1. Combine the bread crumbs, garlic, parsley, 2 tablespoons olive oil, salt, pepper, and dry mustard in a bowl.

2. Remove the stems and cut the tomatoes in half crosswise. Heat the 3 tablespoons olive oil in a large frying pan. Place the tomato halves in the frying pan, cut sides down, and sauté over medium heat for 5 minutes. Carefully turn the tomatoes over and spread about 1 tablespoon of the crumb mixture on each. Turn the heat to low and cook uncovered for about 45 minutes.

SAUTÉED ZUCCHINI FINGERS WITH PARMESAN CHEESE

A tasty, simple way to prepare zucchini for brunch, lunch, or dinner. It also makes a delicious filling for an omelet. — *Irene C. Eilers*

SERVES 4

2 slender medium zucchini

1 tablespoon sweet butter

1 tablespoon olive oil

1 clove garlic, finely minced

2 tablespoons chopped fresh basil

Salt and freshly grated black pepper to taste

½ cup freshly grated Parmesan cheese

1. Cut the zucchini in half and section into fingers approximately 2 inches long by ½ inch wide.

2. Heat the butter and oil in a large skillet over medium-high heat. Add the garlic and sauté for 1 minute. Lower the heat and add the zucchini fingers, tossing to coat them with the garlic. Continue tossing until the fingers are lightly browned and tender but still on the crunchy side.

3. Add the basil, season with salt and pepper, and toss in the Parmesan cheese.

4. Turn off the heat and cover the pan for one minute to give the Parmesan

a chance to soften. Serve immediately with an additional grating of black pepper.

❦
ZUCCHINI AND SUMMER SQUASH SAUTÉ

The fresh herbs, pepper, and vinegar lend a subtle tang to this colorful side dish. — *Frances McDermott*

SERVES 4

> ¼ cup olive oil
> 1 pound zucchini, julienned into 1-inch matchsticks
> 1 pound summer squash, julienned into 1-inch matchsticks
> 1 tablespoon fresh oregano, minced
> 1 tablespoon fresh basil, minced
> 2 tablespoons tarragon vinegar
> Salt and freshly ground black pepper to taste

1. Heat the olive oil in a large, heavy skillet over medium-high heat. Add the zucchini and summer squash and stir-fry quickly for about two minutes.
2. Toss in the fresh herbs, vinegar, salt, and pepper. Sauté another minute, making sure the vegetables retain their color and crispness. Serve immediately with an additional grinding of black pepper.

❦
ANTI-RESTAURANT RICE

One of the things I discovered while working at Blueberry Hill was that most restaurants order from a wholesale supplier and thus end up with many of the same staples. One of these is a blend of wild and white rice, so going out to eat rarely offers surprises in the rice department. It became one of my personal obsessions to do something creative with that rice! Since then I have come to look at rice and other grains as a kind of canvas on which to spread my particular mood of flavors. — *Irene C. Eilers*

SERVES 4

1 tablespoon olive oil

½ cup rice (your favorite; I like basmati, long grain, or a mixture of wild and white)

1½ cups water (amount may vary, depending on the particular variety of rice you choose)

Salt to taste

1. To prepare basic rice, heat the olive oil in a heavy saucepan then add the rice. Stir constantly until the rice is slightly browned. Add the water and salt, bring to a boil, then lower the heat, cover, and simmer on low until the rice is done. (Cooking time varies according to the type of rice used—probably from 25 to 50 minutes.) Serve the rice plain or follow any of these suggestions.

INTERESTING VARIATIONS ON BASIC RICE

Caraway and Black Olive
Sauté caraway seeds and ½ cup chopped onion in the olive oil. Add the rice and cook as in the basic recipe. Toss with sliced black olives and chopped parsley before serving.

Lentil and Spices
Cook 1 cup of lentils separately until barely tender. Drain them and set aside. Sauté ½ cup chopped onion in the olive oil. Add ¼ teaspoon cumin, ⅛ teaspoon cinnamon, and 1 clove garlic pressed through a garlic press. Add the rice and cook as in the basic recipe. Toss in the lentils and reheat if necessary. Chopped tomato adds a nice flavor and color touch.

Watercress and Spice
Sauté the rice in olive oil and add generous pinches of ground cumin, cinnamon, coriander, cardamom, and ginger. Cook as in the basic recipe. Before serving, toss in a large handful of coarsely chopped watercress.

Tomato and Basil
Sauté the rice as in the basic recipe. Add 4 tablespoons of dried basil leaves. Cook as in the basic recipe. Add a generous amount of cubed tomatoes before serving.

❧
Barley Nut Pilaf

I based this recipe on one served to me by my friend Marcia, who always insists "I can't cook." She served this as a side dish to a delicious orange-glazed roast duck. The nutty flavor of the barley, further enhanced by the toasted cashews and almonds, stood up to the richness of the duck. It was the perfect accompaniment to a perfect meal. — *Arlyn Hertz*

SERVES 6

>   4 tablespoons sweet butter
>   1 cup pearl barley, rinsed and drained
>   1 medium onion, finely chopped
>   1 shallot, finely minced
>   2½ cups chicken stock
>   ¾ cup mixed slivered almonds and unsalted cashew pieces, toasted
>   ¼ cup minced fresh parsley
>   Salt and freshly ground black pepper to taste

1. In a large, heavy saucepan, melt the butter over medium-high heat. Add the barley, onions, and shallots and sauté about 5 minutes, until the barley is lightly browned.
2. Stir in the chicken stock and bring to a boil. Cover tightly and lower the heat to a slow simmer. Cook covered about 35 minutes or until the liquid is absorbed and the barley is tender.
3. Toss in the toasted nuts, chopped parsley, salt, and pepper, and serve.

❧
STEAMED RAISIN PUDDING

This is the perfect accompaniment to Roast Fresh Ham, page 86.

— Tory Sneff

SERVES 6

> 2 cups unbleached white flour, sifted
> ¼ cup sweet butter
> 2 eggs
> 1 cup milk
> 2 tablespoons sugar
> Grated rind of 1 lemon
> 1 cup raisins, soaked overnight in 1 cup brandy
> ¼ cup dry bread crumbs

1. In a large bowl, cut the butter into the sifted flour.
2. Beat the eggs with the milk and add to the flour. Stir the mixture well and add the sugar, lemon rind, and brandy-soaked raisins, including any unabsorbed brandy.
3. Butter a pudding mold and dust with the bread crumbs. Pour in the batter and cover the mold. Place the mold in a kettle of boiling water. (The water should reach two-thirds of the way up the mold.) Cover the kettle and steam the pudding for 1½ hours. Add more hot water if necessary to keep the water at the same level.
   Note: If you do not have a pudding mold, use a 1½-quart Pyrex casserole or ovenproof bowl and cover it tightly with aluminum foil.
4. Unmold the pudding on a hot platter and serve with roast fresh ham.

DESSERTS

POPPY SEED CAKE

This moist, golden, poppy-studded cake is a classic dessert. For an extra-special occasion, serve it with a bowl of fresh strawberries and a bowl of whipped cream and let your guests top their own. They're sure to say you've given them the best of all possible worlds. — *Jeanne Eliades*

SERVES 12

1½ cups sweet butter, at room temperature
2 cups sugar
6 eggs, lightly beaten
3 tablespoons grated lemon rind
1 tablespoon grated orange rind
1 teaspoon vanilla extract
¾ cup poppy seeds
2 cups plus 2 tablespoons unbleached white flour
2 teaspoons baking powder
¾ teaspoon salt
¾ cup plus 2 tablespoons milk
2 tablespoons freshly squeezed orange juice
¼ cup freshly squeezed lemon juice
¼ cup sugar

1. Preheat the oven to 350°. Grease a 10-inch bundt pan.

2. In a large mixing bowl, cream together for 2 minutes the butter and 2 cups sugar. Add the eggs, lemon and orange rinds, and vanilla, and continue to beat another 2 minutes.

3. In a separate bowl, mix together the poppy seeds, flour, baking powder, and salt. Add this alternately with the milk to the butter-egg mixture, beginning and ending with the dry ingredients. Mix until well blended and smooth.

4. Bake the cake for 1 hour, or until a cake tester or toothpick comes out clean when inserted into the middle of the cake. Remove from the oven and let cool in the pan on a wire rack.

5. Prepare the glaze: stir together the orange juice, lemon juice, and ¼ cup of sugar. While the cake is still cooling in the pan, prick holes in the top (a toothpick works well) and drizzle the glaze evenly over the cake.

6. Remove the cake to a platter when it has cooled and all the glaze is absorbed.

LIME PIE
IN MERINGUE CRUST

A light, airy, and tart dessert. The meringue crust and lime custard are a heavenly combination. Allow for seconds, or at least be prepared to allow your guests to lick the pie plate. — *Arlyn Hertz*

SERVES 8

> 5 egg whites, at room temperature
> ¼ teaspoon cream of tartar
> ¾ cup sugar
> 5 egg yolks
> ⅛ teaspoon salt
> ⅓ cup sugar
> ⅓ cup freshly squeezed lime juice
> 2 tablespoons grated lime peel
> 2 cups whipping cream, divided in half
> Lime slices for garnish

1. Preheat the oven to 275°. Grease a 10-inch pie plate and set it aside.

2. In a large bowl, beat the egg whites with the cream of tartar until soft peaks form. Slowly add ¾ cup sugar, a little at a time, beating until stiff and glossy.

3. Spoon the meringue into the prepared pie plate, mounding it up the sides and over the edge. Bake one hour and cool at room temperature.

4. To prepare the filling: beat the egg yolks and salt in a medium-size bowl until fluffy. Whisk in ⅓ cup sugar, lime juice, and peel, and place the mixture in the top of a double boiler over boiling water. Whisk constantly until thick and smooth, about 10 minutes. Remove from the heat and let cool.

5. Beat one cup of the cream until stiff. Fold this into the cooled lime custard and pour into the cooled meringue shell. Refrigerate the pie at least 4 hours. Serve garnished with the additional cup of cream, whipped, and lime slices.

❦
BLUEBERRY GATEAU

Blueberry gateau at Blueberry Hill—a classic. Serve it warm with a dollop of Cassis-flavored whipped cream, or plain at teatime. — *Arlyn Hertz*

SERVES 8

½ cup sweet butter at room temperature

1 cup sugar

1 cup unbleached white flour

1 teaspoon baking powder

Pinch of salt

2 eggs

3 cups blueberries, picked over, washed, and drained

2 tablespoons sugar

2 tablespoons freshly squeezed lemon juice

1 tablespoon unbleached white flour

1. Preheat the oven to 350°. Lightly butter a 9-inch springform pan. Set aside.
2. In a large bowl, cream the butter with 1 cup of sugar until light and fluffy.
3. In another bowl, mix together the flour, baking powder, and salt. Beat this into the butter mixture. Beat in the eggs, one at a time.
4. Place the batter in the prepared springform pan.
5. Toss the berries with the 2 tablespoons sugar, lemon juice, and 1 tablespoon of flour. Spread evenly over the top of the batter.
6. Bake 1 hour. Cool in the pan. Remove the sides of the pan and turn onto a cake plate, berry side up.

❦
GINGER SNAPS

These spicy cookies were my childhood favorites, so the recipe has special memories for me. I began baking these at the inn before a cookie jar ever existed there, but it didn't matter—the guests smelled them baking, appeared in the kitchen, and ate them as soon as they came out of the oven.

— *Elsie Sherrill*

MAKES ABOUT 30 COOKIES

1 cup sugar
1 egg
¾ cup vegetable oil
¼ cup molasses
2 cups unbleached white flour
2 teaspoons baking soda
¼ teaspoon salt
1 teaspoon cinnamon
½ teaspoon ground ginger
½ teaspoon ground cloves
Sugar for rolling cookies

1. Preheat the oven to 350°. Lightly grease a cookie sheet.
2. In a mixing bowl, cream together the sugar, egg, oil, and molasses.
3. Combine the flour, soda, salt, cinnamon, ginger, and cloves and add it to the creamed mixture. Mix well.
4. Form into 1-inch balls. Roll the balls in sugar and place, about 2 inches apart, on the greased cookie sheet.
5. Bake for 10 to 12 minutes. Remove from the oven and cool on a rack. Store in tightly sealed jar.

❦

STRAWBERRY MERINGUE TORTE

Celebrate the strawberry season with this luscious dessert. — *Arlyn Hertz*

SERVES 8

7 egg whites, at room temperature
1½ cups sugar
2 tablespoons vinegar
1 teaspoon vanilla extract
2 pints fresh strawberries, picked over, washed, and sliced
1 pint whipping cream
8 whole strawberries for garnish

1. Preheat the oven to 275°. Butter the bottom *only* of a 10-inch springform pan. Set aside.
2. Beat the egg whites until very stiff and glossy. Gradually beat in the sugar, a little at a time. Beat in the vinegar, then vanilla.

3. Heap the meringue into the prepared springform pan. Smooth the top. Bake 1¼ hours, or until the meringue is firm and lightly browned. Immediately remove the sides of the springform pan. Remove the top of the crust carefully in large pieces and set aside. Let cool.

4. Whip the cream until soft peaks form. Set aside enough (about 1 cup) for garnish. Fold the remaining whipped cream into the berries. Spoon the berry/cream mixture into the meringue bottom. Replace the top crust pieces. Refrigerate torte at least 2 hours. Serve each piece garnished with a dollop of whipped cream and a whole strawberry.

❦

LEMON TART

The filling is velvet-smooth and refreshingly tart—a perfect summer dessert. As a change, instead of one large tart or pie, try making them as eight individual tartlets. — *Jeanne Eliades*

SERVES 8

> 4 large lemons
> 3 eggs
> 6 egg yolks
> ½ cup sugar
> ½ teaspoon salt
> 10 tablespoons sweet butter
> 9-inch prebaked tart shell (see recipe for Sugar Tart Crust on page 156)
> 1 cup heavy cream, whipped, for garnish
> Fresh mint sprigs, for garnish

1. To make the lemon curd: using a rinder, remove the rind from the lemons, then chop rind finely. (Or you can grate the rind off the lemons, being careful not to take any of the pith.) Juice the 4 lemons.

2. In the top of a double boiler, place the eggs and the egg yolks and beat well with a whisk. Add the sugar, lemon juice, rind, and salt, and combine with the whisk. Cook over barely simmering water, whisking constantly, until the mixture thickens, about 3 to 5 minutes.

3. Remove from the heat and stir in the butter, 2 tablespoons at a time, until it melts and the mixture is well combined. Set aside until it is completely cooled.

4. Once cooled, pour lemon curd into cooked tart shell and refrigerate for at least 3 hours. Serve cold, garnished with whipped cream and fresh sprigs of mint.

LATTICED PEACH-BLUEBERRY PIE

What is better than peaches and cream? Blueberry peach pie served with whipped cream, that's what! I'm really proud of this creation, almost as proud as when a ski trail was named for me: Elsie's Loop. — *Elsie Sherrill*

SERVES 8

> 1 unbaked piecrust, enough for a double crust, 10-inch pie
> (see recipe on page 155)
> 3 cups blueberries, picked over and washed
> 2 cups fresh peaches, peeled and sliced
> ¾ cup sugar
> 3 tablespoons cornstarch
> ¼ teaspoon cinnamon
> ½ teaspoon grated lemon rind
> 1 tablespoon half and half
> Whipped cream or vanilla ice cream

1. Preheat the oven to 375°.
2. Roll out half of the pie crust on a lightly floured surface and line a 10-inch pie plate with it. Trim and crimp the edges. Place the other half of the pie crust in the refrigerator until ready to use.
3. Place the blueberries and peaches in a large bowl. Combine the sugar, cornstarch, and cinnamon and toss with the fruit. Add the grated lemon rind and toss again.
4. Place the filling in the unbaked pie shell. Roll out the other half of the pie crust between two sheets of waxed paper to form a 12-inch circle. Cut in ½-inch strips and place them lattice fashion over the pie filling. Trim the ends and crimp the edge of the crust decoratively. Brush lattice with the half and half.
5. Bake the pie on the middle rack of the oven about 40 minutes, or until the filling is bubbling and the crust is lightly browned.
6. Remove from the oven and let cool before slicing. Serve with a generous dollop of whipped cream or a scoop of vanilla ice cream.

STRAWBERRY-RHUBARB CRISP
WITH ALMOND CHANTILLY CREAM

There's no substitute for fresh local strawberries, so make this dessert when they are in season and plentiful. — *Frances McDermott*

SERVES 8

4 cups diced rhubarb
5 cups strawberries, stemmed and diced
1 cup granulated sugar
1 tablespoon grated orange rind
2 tablespoons cornstarch
⅓ cup Grand Marnier
¾ cup sweet butter, cut into small pieces
2 cups unbleached white flour
1 cup old fashioned rolled oats
¾ cup packed brown sugar
1 tablespoon cinnamon
¾ cup slivered almonds
Pinch of salt
1 egg, lightly beaten
2 cups heavy whipping cream
1 to 2 tablespoons confectioners' sugar
1 to 2 teaspoons almond extract

1. Preheat the oven to 350°. Lightly butter the bottom of a 4-quart baking dish.

2. In a large bowl, toss the rhubarb and strawberries with the granulated sugar and orange zest.

3. Dissolve the cornstarch in the Grand Marnier and toss with the fruit mixture so that it is well coated. Spoon into the prepared baking dish.

4. Place the butter, flour, oats, brown sugar, and cinnamon in a mixing bowl. Mix with your hands or a pastry cutter until it is crumbly. Stir in the almonds and salt, and stir in the beaten egg with a fork to bind the mixture. Spread it evenly over the strawberries and rhubarb.

5. Bake the crisp for 45 minutes or until the top is nicely browned and the mixture is bubbling. Remove from the oven and keep warm.

6. Whip the cream with the confectioners' sugar to the soft-peak stage. Whip in the almond extract. Serve in generous dollops on the warm crisp.

❦
ANANAS AU CHOCOLAT
(PINEAPPLE WITH CHOCOLATE SAUCE)

This dessert is a perfect example of simple elegance: ripe pineapple served with a warm, smooth, chocolate sauce. It's wonderful. It's easy. And it's still a favorite of Tony's—so much so that toward the end of every season we have to put a ban on his serving it. — *Laurie Taylor*

SERVES 4

> 1 ripe pineapple
> 5 squares bittersweet chocolate
> 2 tablespoons strong brewed coffee
> ¾ cup heavy cream
> 1 tablespoon sweet butter
> 2 tablespoons Grand Marnier or Cointreau
> 1 kiwi fruit, peeled and sliced
> 4 large strawberries, washed and cut in half

1. Slice one inch from the bottom of the pineapple. Cut the pineapple in half lengthwise, leaving the crown of leaves. Cut each half lengthwise so that there are 4 long wedges, each with its share of leaves.

2. Slice off the hard center core of each wedge. Sever the pineapple from the peel. Put the wedges back on the peel and make bite-size crosswise cuts.

3. Melt the chocolate in a double boiler over hot (not boiling) water. Stir in the coffee and mix well. Stirring constantly, whisk in the butter, cream, and Grand Marnier or Cointreau. Continue to cook and stir for about 5 minutes or until the sauce is slightly thickened.

4. Place each pineapple wedge on a separate plate, drizzle with the warm chocolate sauce, and garnish with the kiwi and strawberry slices.

❧
RASPBERRY CRÊPES

This is a great last-minute dessert that looks much more elaborate than it actually is to prepare, especially if you have a supply of previously frozen crêpes on hand. However, fresh raspberries are a must. I served this on red glass dessert plates and it looked truly spectacular. — *Elsie Sherrill*

SERVES 6

> 8 ounces cream cheese at room temperature
> ⅓ cup confectioners' sugar
> Grated rind of 1 lemon
> ½ teaspoon vanilla extract
> 1 cup heavy cream, whipped to soft peaks
> 6 crêpes (see recipe for Basic Crêpes on page 157)
> 1 pint fresh raspberries, rinsed and picked over
> 2 tablespoons Framboise (optional)

1. In a medium bowl, whip together the cream cheese, confectioners' sugar, lemon rind, and vanilla until the mixture is smooth and fluffy.
2. Fold half of the whipped cream gently into the mixture until well combined.
3. To assemble, lay each crêpe on a dessert plate. Spoon about ¼ cup of the cream cheese mixture down the middle of each crêpe, sprinkle a few raspberries on the cream cheese, then fold the crêpe by bringing both sides towards the center. Spoon the remaining whipped cream on top of each folded crêpe and toss on the remaining berries. Drizzle a little Framboise over each crêpe, if desired. Serve immediately.

❧
LIME CHEESECAKE

This is one of my all-time favorite cheesecakes, and has pleased many friends and guests over the years. There is nothing quite as satisfying as having a guest ask for the recipe, or for cake leftovers before breakfast. — *Irene C. Eilers*

SERVES 10

Crust

- 1 cup graham cracker crumbs (or the equivalent of any favorite cookie. I've had great success with Blueberry Hill chocolate chip cookies.)
- 2 tablespoons sugar
- 1 generous pinch each of cardamom and cinnamon
- ¼ cup melted sweet butter

Filling

- 3 8-ounce packages of cream cheese, softened
- 3 eggs
- 1 cup sugar
- ¼ cup freshly squeezed lime juice (about 2 limes)
- 2 tablespoons grated lime rind
- ⅛ teaspoon vanilla extract

Topping

- 1½ cups dairy sour cream
- 2 tablespoons sugar
- 1 tablespoon freshly squeezed lime juice
- ⅛ teaspoon vanilla extract (optional)

Garnish

- 1 kiwi fruit peeled and thinly sliced, or 1 lime thinly sliced

FOR THE CRUST

1. Preheat the oven to 350°.
2. Combine all the crust ingredients and press into the bottom of a 9-inch springform pan. Bake for 5 minutes. Remove from the oven and cool. Lower oven temperature to 250°.

FOR THE FILLING

3. In a large bowl, with an electric mixer set on medium speed, beat the cream cheese with the eggs, alternating cream cheese with egg, beating well after each addition.
4. Gradually add the sugar alternately with the lime juice. Beat an additional 10 minutes at medium speed. Add the grated lime rind and vanilla extract and continue to mix at medium speed for 2 minutes more.
5. Pour filling into cooled crust and bake at 250° for 25 minutes. Turn off the heat and leave the cake in the oven for another 45 minutes. Remove cheesecake from the oven and keep at room temperature while preparing the topping.

FOR THE TOPPING

6. Combine all the ingredients and keep topping at room temperature until ready to spread on cheesecake.

7. Preheat the oven to 350°.

8. Gently spread the topping evenly over the warm cheesecake. Return the cake to the preheated oven and bake for 10 minutes. Remove and cool on a wire rack.

9. Refrigerate for several hours or overnight before removing from the springform pan. To serve, remove the sides of the pan and decorate the cake with thinly sliced kiwi or lime slices.

❦

ABSOLUTELY THE
BEST CREAM-CHEESE CAKE

This recipe has been passed down through the Sneff family tree. I absolutely love it. You have to blend the cream cheese mixture for 30 minutes, so it helps if you have a standing mixer—and perhaps someone to spell you. — *Tory Sneff*

SERVES 10 TO 12

> 2¼ pounds cream cheese (a bit more than four
>   8-ounce packages)
> 1½ cups sugar
> 4 eggs
> 2 teaspoons vanilla extract
> 2 teaspoons lemon juice
> 12 double graham crackers
> ¼ pound melted sweet butter
> Fresh blueberries or strawberries for garnish
> Fresh mint sprigs for garnish

1. In the bowl of a standing mixer, mix together the cream cheese, sugar, eggs, vanilla, and lemon juice for 30 minutes. Mixture should be ultra smooth.

2. Preheat the oven to 350°.

3. While mixing the cheese, crush the graham crackers and mix with the melted butter. Line a 9-inch springform pan with the cracker mixture. Add the cheese filling.

4. Bake the cake for 45 minutes. Remove from the oven and let cool in the pan on a wire rack. Remove the sides of the pan.

5. Refrigerate the cake if you are not serving it immediately. When ready to serve, garnish with fresh berries and mint sprigs.

❦

Fresh Fruit
and White Velvet Parfait

Rich, velvety smooth, delicious, and simple. — *Arlyn Hertz*

SERVES 8

> 2 cups whipping cream
> ½ cup sugar
> Dash of salt
> 1 tablespoon unflavored gelatin dissolved in 2 tablespoons cold water
> 2 cups sour cream
> 2 cups fresh strawberries (or raspberries) picked over, washed, hulled, and sliced
> 8 whole berries for garnish
> Fresh mint sprigs for garnish

1. In a large saucepan, heat the cream until it bubbles. Stir in the sugar and salt. Remove from heat.

2. Add the softened gelatin to the cream and stir until it is dissolved. Add the sour cream and stir until well blended. Let cool.

3. In parfait glasses, spoon a layer of the cream mixture, then a layer of the berries, then a layer of the cream mixture.

4. Refrigerate the parfaits for 2 hours or until firm. Garnish each parfait with a whole strawberry and a fresh mint sprig.

❦
BLUEBERRIES IN MAPLE CREAM

This recipe was created one hectic evening when I was in need of a quick dessert. It is so good and so simple. John Ogden, then a Blueberry Hill waiter and, like me, a "ski bum," was at my side for moral support and taste testing, and we managed to eat several quarts of this dessert in the process before serving it to the guests. It made a big hit and still never fails to do so.

— Alan Levy

SERVES 6

> 6 cups fresh blueberries, picked over and washed
> 3 cups heavy cream
> ⅓ to ½ cup Vermont maple syrup

1. At 6:00 A.M., send someone out into the blueberry bushes to pick 6 cups of dew-covered blueberries; chill until dessert time. Or, visit your local farm stand at a more civilized hour.
2. At dessert time, thoroughly blend the heavy cream with the maple syrup. The maple flavor should emerge as a subtle aftertaste.
3. Divide the berries into 1-cup portions and pour ½ cup of the maple cream over each portion.
4. Eat 2 portions in the kitchen and serve the other 4.

❦
ORANGES GRAND MARNIER

A truly sophisticated dessert. *— Tory Sneff*

SERVES 8

> 8 oranges
> 2 lemons
> 3 cups water
> 1½ cups sugar
> 2 cups white wine
> 5 tablespoons Grand Marnier
> 3 tablespoons white wine

1. Using a sharp knife or a vegetable peeler peel the skin in thin strips (about ¼ inch wide) from the oranges, being careful not to get any of the white pith. Set the peel aside. Peel the remaining skin and pith from the oranges, hollow out any pith from the center, and set oranges on a platter, opening each into a "flower" while keeping all the sections intact.

2. Peel the skin from the lemons in thin strips, being careful not to get any white pith.

3. In a heavy saucepan, bring the water to a boil. Add the orange and lemon peels and boil for 5 minutes. Drain and set aside.

4. In another saucepan, combine the sugar and the 2 cups white wine. Cook over medium-low heat until the sugar dissolves. Increase the heat to high and boil until syrup becomes caramel color.

5. Remove syrup from the heat and stir in the Grand Marnier and 3 tablespoons of white wine. Pour the syrup over the oranges. Mound the peels on top of the oranges and over the syrup around the fruit.

❦

CHAMPAGNE-POACHED PEARS

I served this light, refreshing dessert often as the grand finale to a heavy meal. It's also a nice dish to serve at a brunch. — *Laurie Taylor*

SERVES 4

> 4 ripe Bartlett or Anjou pears
> 1 bottle champagne, not too dry
> ½ cup sugar
> 1 orange, quartered
> 1 tablespoon essence of orange extract
> 1 tablespoon whole cloves
> 1 orange, sliced thin, for garnish
> 4 sprigs fresh mint for garnish

1. Peel, halve, and core the pears and place them in a large nonreactive saucepan. Add the champagne, sugar, orange quarters, essence of orange, and cloves.

2. Bring the pears to a gentle boil. Reduce the heat and simmer, covered, until pears are barely tender. (This may take from ½ to 1 hour, depending on the ripeness of the pears.) Remove the pan from the heat and bring the pears and liquid to room temperature.

3. Place the pears and liquid in the refrigerator and chill for at least 1 hour. Serve pears with some of the liquid spooned over them and garnish with an orange slice and sprig of mint.

🍐

POACHED PEARS

A great way to end an elegant dinner party, and so easy to make. Use up all those leftover pears in the fruit bowl! — *Tony Clark*

SERVES 6

> 6 Anjou pears, ripe yet firm
> 3 cups red Bordeaux wine
> 1 cup sugar
> 1 cinnamon stick, 2 inches
> 1 orange, sliced
> 1 lemon, sliced
> 1 grapefruit, sliced
> 1 lime, sliced
> 1 cup heavy cream, whipped to soft peaks
> Mint leaves for garnish

1. Peel the pears, leaving the stem on the fruit.
2. Pour the wine in a nonreactive kettle large enough to hold the pears in a single layer. Stir in the sugar and cinnamon stick and bring to a simmer. Place the pears upright in the wine. Add the sliced fruit and enough liquid so that the pears are three-quarters submerged. Cover tightly and simmer until pears are soft, but not limp. Cooking time will be anywhere from 30 minutes to more than 1 hour, depending on the ripeness of the pears.
3. Remove the pears from the cooking liquid and let them cool on a sheet pan. (By the way, the cooking liquid makes an excellent hot spiced wine drink.)
4. Once cooled, core the pears but save 1 inch of the core with the stem.
5. Using a pastry bag with a decorative tip, pipe a circle of whipped cream onto each plate. Place a pear in the circle, then fill the cavity in the pear with more whipped cream. Replace the piece of core with the stem, then garnish with a mint leaf.

❦
THEATRICAL RASPBERRIES
AND ICE CREAM

I was treated to this goody during a theater intermission in Munich, and it's been a wonderful standby for me ever since. If you have a good chilled champagne on hand, serve it too. — *Irene C. Eilers*

SERVES 4

> 1 package frozen raspberries in syrup, thawed
> 1 pint vanilla ice cream, the best you can find, or better yet, use the recipe on page 148
> 4 tablespoons Cointreau

1. Heat the raspberries in a small saucepan until warmed through, but don't boil.
2. Scoop the ice cream into 4 champagne glasses. Top each with warm raspberry sauce and 1 tablespoon Cointreau. Serve immediately.

❦
ORANGE MOUSSE

This is a light and elegant finale to a rich meal. Fresh orange juice is available 12 months of the year—juice from concentrate just won't do—so it's a year-round dessert treat. — *Lynn Levy*

SERVES 8

> 8 tablespoons sweet butter
> 5 eggs
> ⅔ cup granulated sugar
> ¾ cup *fresh* orange juice
> Grated zest of 3 oranges
> 3 cups heavy cream, chilled
> 8 mint leaves, for garnish

1. Melt the butter in the top part of a double boiler over simmering, not boiling, water.
2. Beat the eggs and sugar in a bowl until they are light and foamy. Add them to the melted butter and cook gently, stirring constantly, until the mixture becomes a custard, about 8 minutes. Do not overcook or you will end up with scrambled eggs.

3. Remove the custard from the heat and stir in the orange juice and grated zest. Cool to room temperature.

4. Whip the cream until it forms very stiff peaks.

5. Stir the orange custard into the whipped cream until just incorporated. Pour into 8 individual serving glasses and chill for at least 4 hours. Serve garnished with fresh mint leaves.

❧

STRAWBERRY MOUSSE

Weddings at Blueberry Hill are definitely something personal and special. Strawberry mousse was requested by one couple for their rehearsal dinner at the inn, so I tried out a couple of different recipes and came up with this one.
— *Frances McDermott*

SERVES 6 TO 8

1 quart strawberries, washed and hulled

6 tablespoons confectioners' sugar

1 tablespoon lemon juice

3 tablespoons Fraise, Framboise or Cassis

1¼ cups heavy cream

3 egg whites

Whole strawberries and mint sprigs for garnish

1. In a food processor fitted with a steel blade, purée the strawberries. Add the sugar and lemon juice and process just until combined.

2. Transfer the berry mixture to a large nonreactive saucepan and cook over low heat until the mixture is reduced to about one cup. Stir frequently, taking care that the berries do not stick to the bottom of the pan. Remove from the heat, transfer to a bowl, and chill well.

3. When chilled, whisk the liqueur into the purée.

4. Whip the cream so that it forms soft peaks. Set aside.

5. Whip the egg whites until they are stiff. Set aside.

6. Fold the whipped cream into the berry purée, then fold in ⅓ of the whites. Carefully fold in the remainder of the whites.

7. Ladle the mousse into chilled glasses and chill about 4 hours or overnight. Serve well chilled, garnished with a fresh whole strawberry and mint sprig.

BISQUE TORTONI

This Italian classic, a cross between ice cream and mousse, is a delightful light dessert, perfect after a heavy meal. — *Arlyn Hertz*

SERVES 8 TO 10

> 2 egg whites at room temperature
> ½ cup confectioners' sugar
> 1 pint whipping cream
> 1 teaspoon vanilla extract
> 3 tablespoons sherry or Marsala
> ½ teaspoon almond extract
> ¾ cup toasted unsweetened coconut

1. Beat the egg whites until stiff and glossy. Gradually beat in ¼ cup of the sugar. Set aside.
2. Whip the cream until thick. Whip in the remaining ¼ cup of sugar, the vanilla, sherry, and almond extract. Beat until soft peaks form. Fold in ½ cup of the coconut. Fold in the egg whites.
3. Divide the mixture evenly among dessert glasses. Garnish with the remaining coconut. Place in the freezer until frozen. Remove 5 to 10 minutes before serving.

FROZEN SOUFFLÉ WITH VANILLA CRÈME ANGLAISE AND RASPBERRY SAUCE

A frozen soufflé is a quick and easy substitute for ice cream if you don't have an ice-cream maker. The texture is lighter, the flavor is wonderful, and the crème anglaise adds the requisite creaminess. You should note that the liqueur in the soufflé acts like "antifreeze," so allow ample time for the soufflé to freeze. — *Frances McDermott*

SERVES 4 TO 6

Soufflé

2 cups whipping cream

¼ to ½ cup sugar (depending on the sweetness of the liqueur you choose)

3 whole eggs

2 egg yolks

6 tablespoons of your favorite liqueur (I use Grand Marnier)

Crème Anglaise

1 cup light cream or milk

4 egg yolks

⅓ cup sugar

Pinch of salt

½ teaspoon vanilla extract

Raspberry Sauce

1 pint fresh raspberries

Juice of ½ lemon

½ cup sugar

¼ cup water

2 tablespoons Chambord (optional)

Garnish

½ pint raspberries

Fresh mint leaves

FOR THE SOUFFLÉ

1. Whip the cream until it forms soft peaks and set aside in the refrigerator.

2. Over low heat, using a hand-held electric mixer, beat the sugar, eggs, and egg yolks until warm to the touch and doubled in volume. Remove from the heat and add the liqueur. Continue beating over a bowl of ice and water until cold. Gently fold in the whipped cream. Place in the freezer until well frozen.

FOR THE CRÈME ANGLAISE

3. Scald the milk or cream and set aside to cool slightly.

4. Lightly beat the egg yolks, sugar, and salt. Add the milk or cream in a slow, steady stream, whisking to incorporate. Place over low heat, stirring constantly until the mixture thickens and coats the back of a wooden spoon.

5. Add the vanilla, strain, and cool in the refrigerator. Bring back to room temperature when ready to serve.

FOR THE RASPBERRY SAUCE

6. In a food processor fitted with a steel blade, combine the raspberries, lemon juice, and water. Purée and strain to remove seeds.

7. In a saucepan, combine the purée with the sugar and bring to a boil over moderately high heat. Simmer for 15 minutes. Remove from the heat and add the Chambord. Refrigerate until ready to use.

TO SERVE

8. Sauce each individual dessert plate with a spoonful of the crème anglaise to cover the base of the plate. Add a small amount of the raspberry sauce and swirl throughout the crème. Using a small scoop, place 2 scoops of frozen soufflé on the plate. Garnish with fresh raspberries and mint leaves.

KIWI AND HONEYDEW SORBET

Pale and green and very refreshing. Definitely a summertime treat!

— Alan Levy

MAKES ABOUT 1 QUART

1 large ripe honeydew melon

3 ripe kiwis

⅔ cup sugar

¼ cup freshly squeezed lemon juice

⅓ cup heavy cream

2 tablespoons Framboise liqueur

1. Remove the rind and seeds from the honeydew and cut up into bite-size pieces.

2. Peel the kiwi and cut in half.

3. Place the fruit in a food processor fitted with a steel blade. Add the sugar and lemon juice and process until smooth. Pour in the cream and Framboise and process until blended.

4. Place mixture in an ice-cream maker and freeze, following the directions for your particular ice-cream maker.

Jeanne's Vanilla Ice Cream

This is the real thing—pure, delicious, and unadulterated vanilla ice cream.

— *Jeanne Eliades*

MAKES 2 QUARTS

>1 vanilla bean
>3 cups heavy cream
>3 cups milk
>14 egg yolks
>1¼ cups sugar

1. Scrape out the seeds of the vanilla bean and discard the seeds. Chop the pod.
2. In a large heavy saucepan, bring to a boil the cream, milk, and chopped vanilla bean. As soon as it boils, remove from the heat and let cool. Once the mixture has cooled, process it in a blender so that the bean is ground up. Strain the mixture to remove any large particles.
3. Put the 14 eggs yolks and 1¼ cups sugar in the same saucepan used for the cream and milk. Whisk well until light and pale yellow. Return the cream and milk to the egg mixture and put over medium heat. Whisk constantly until the mixture coats the back of a spoon, about 5 minutes. Strain again.
4. Cool the mixture in the refrigerator. When completely cool, pour into an ice cream freezer and follow the directions for the particular ice cream freezer you're using.

Chocolate Ganache

Nothing could be simpler for a last-minute dessert. It's rich and chocolate. Ganache can be poured over ice cream or pound cake or drizzled over fresh fruit. It also makes a wonderful icing. For a special taste combination, try pouring the warm ganache over chilled poached pears. — *Elsie Sherrill*

MAKES ABOUT 3 CUPS

>2 cups heavy cream
>16 ounces semi-sweet chocolate, chopped

1. In a medium saucepan, bring the cream to a full boil. Remove the pan from the heat.

2. Add in the chopped chocolate and let it sit for 1 minute. Stir the mixture with a wire whisk until the chocolate has melted and the ganache is totally smooth.

SAUCES
&
MISCELLANEOUS

BLUEBERRY CHAMPAGNE VINEGAR

With the plethora of blueberries found at Blueberry Hill, it's only natural and fitting tht one creative use for them would be to make a vinegar. This vinegar has a light, slightly fruity taste, perfect for salad dressings, mayonnaise, and sauces. — *Laurie Taylor*

MAKES 3 CUPS

> ½ cup fresh blueberries, washed and drained
> 2 pieces (1 inch each) of stick cinnamon
> 1 1-inch by ¼-inch strip of orange zest
> 2 cups white vinegar
> ½ cup champagne
> 1 tablespoon honey

1. Place the blueberries, cinnamon, and orange zest in a sterilized bottle large enough to hold 3 cups of liquid.
2. In a medium saucepan, heat the vinegar, champagne, and honey until the mixture is simmering, and simmer for 2 minutes.
3. Pour the mixture into the bottle with the berries and cinnamon. Cap tightly and place in a cool, dark place. Allow vinegar to sit for at least two weeks. If you're not going to use the vinegar right away, you may want to strain it before storing it longer.

BLUEBERRY MAYONNAISE

Serve this mayonnaise as an alternative dressing with chilled artichokes (see recipe on page 47). It's also wonderful with a fresh salad of crabmeat or other seafood. This mayonnaise is so superior to any commercial product that once you've tried it and you see how simple it is to make, you'll never want to use the "store-bought" variety again. It will keep for about 1 week refrigerated in a tightly sealed container. — *Laurie Taylor*

MAKES ABOUT 2 CUPS

1 whole egg
2 egg yolks
1 tablespoon Dijon mustard
1 tablespoon sherry
¼ cup Blueberry Champagne Vinegar (see recipe on page 152)
Salt and freshly ground white pepper to taste
1 cup olive oil
1 cup corn or salad oil
¼ cup chopped fresh scallions

1. Place the egg and egg yolks, mustard, sherry, vinegar, salt, and pepper in the bowl of a food processor fitted with a steel blade. Blend until the mixture is lemon colored.
2. With the motor running, *slowly* add the oils. (If you add them too quickly the mayonnaise will break.) When all the oil is incorporated, pulse in the scallions. Refrigerate the mayonnaise.

❦

Salsa Cruda

It's important to use ripe tomatoes. If they're unavailable, I think it's better to substitute good quality canned tomatoes rather than pale and tasteless fresh ones. — *Jeanne Eliades*

MAKES 2 TO 3 CUPS

1 small white onion (or yellow, if white isn't available)
1 large clove garlic
1 jalapeño chili, seeded
½ bunch cilantro, washed and dried
5 ripe tomatoes
1 tablespoon fresh lime juice
Salt and freshly ground black pepper to taste

1. Mince the onion, garlic and chili.
2. Pull the cilantro leaves from the stems, and chop the leaves coarsely.
3. Chop the tomatoes coarsely.
4. Combine all ingredients in a large glass bowl; add the lime juice and the salt and pepper to taste. Transfer to a tightly covered container. Keeps in the refrigerator for up to a week.

PESTO SAUCE

Not very often do we allow a guest to take over the kitchen, but Blueberry Hill guest Jeff Kruh decided to join me in putting out a breakfast for 25 people one morning. His scrambled eggs with pesto sauce were an immediate hit. He merely stirred 2 tablespoons of the pesto sauce into each serving of almost-set scrambled eggs, finished cooking them, and *voila!* Here's the recipe for his pesto sauce. It's more than you'll need for scrambled eggs (unless you're planning on serving 25 people), but the leftovers are great over pasta. Just add more olive oil until you get the desired consistency. — *Tony Clark*

MAKES ABOUT 1½ CUPS

> 1 cup walnuts, lightly toasted
> 1 cup pine nuts, lightly toasted
> 2 cups fresh basil leaves, packed
> 1 cup fresh parsley leaves, packed
> 20 cloves garlic
> 1 cup extra-virgin olive oil
> 1½ cups grated Parmesan cheese
> Salt and freshly ground black pepper to taste

1. In a food processor fitted with a steel blade, coarsely chop the walnuts and the pine nuts and set them aside in a bowl.
2. Place the basil and parsley in the food processor. Process until coarsely chopped, but do not purée—it should be the consistency of oatmeal. Pulse the garlic into the basil-parsley mixture and remove to a medium-size bowl.
3. With a fork, mix in the nuts, Parmesan cheese, salt, and pepper. Store in a tightly sealed container in the refrigerator.

RAISIN SAUCE

I served this simple sauce as an accompaniment to fresh ham, lamb, and turkey. However, the guests also loved it the next morning on their toast.

— *Elsie Sherrill*

MAKES ABOUT 2 CUPS

2 tablespoons fresh lemon juice
1 tablespoon cornstarch
1 cup orange marmalade
1 box (1 pound) seedless raisins
Grated rind of 1 lemon
⅔ cup chopped walnuts

1. Dissolve the cornstarch in the lemon juice.
2. Place the marmalade in a heavy saucepan over medium heat. Stir constantly until the marmalade becomes liquidy, then lower the heat and stir in the cornstarch mixture.
3. Add the raisins, lemon rind, and nuts and continue to cook over low heat, stirring occasionally, until the sauce comes clear, about 20 minutes.
4. Remove the sauce from the heat and allow it to come to room temperature. Store in a tightly sealed container in the refrigerator. Serve the sauce at room temperature.

❦
PIECRUST

This reliable piecrust was passed down through the Caswell family. The fresh lemon juice gives the crust a unique flavor. Try substituting fresh orange or lime juice for a subtle variation. — *Laurie Caswell*

MAKES TWO 10-INCH PIECRUSTS

2¼ cups unbleached white flour
½ teaspoon salt
1 teaspoon sugar
8 tablespoons (1 stick) sweet butter, chilled and cut into small pieces
6 tablespoons solid vegetable shortening, chilled and cut into small pieces
1 tablespoon fresh lemon juice
5 tablespoons ice water

1. Sift the dry ingredients into a bowl. With a pastry blender or a mixer, blend in the chilled butter and shortening, working quickly, until pieces are the size of small peas.

2. Combine the lemon juice and ice water. Add just enough of the mixture to the dough to hold it together. Turn onto a lightly floured surface and knead gently for a few seconds.

3. Divide the dough and form each half into a ball. Wrap in plastic and refrigerate at least 2 hours or until ready to use. Roll out and bake according to your favorite recipe.

❦
PÂTE BRISÉE

This crust is perfect for quiches or cheese tarts. It's basic and simple—at least that's what my mother, Mary, told me when she gave me the recipe. And, once again, Mother was right. — *Tony Clark*

MAKES ONE 10-INCH CRUST

> 1¼ cups unbleached white flour
> ¼ teaspoon salt
> 6 tablespoons (¾ stick) sweet butter, chilled and broken into small pieces
> 1 tablespoon ice water
> 1 egg yolk

1. Sift the flour and salt into a mixing bowl. Add the butter and blend lightly with your fingertips or pastry blender until the mixture resembles coarse meal.

2. In a separate bowl, beat the egg yolk while slowly adding the ice water. Drizzle this over the dough and work in gently with your fingertips.

3. Press the dough into a ball and knead lightly 2 or 3 times. Form it into a ball again, wrap it in plastic, and refrigerate for at least 2 hours or until ready to use.

4. Use the dough according to your recipe.

❦
SUGAR TART CRUST

Arlyn Hertz gave me this recipe when I first worked at Blueberry Hill as her prep cook. I was a novice at baking but she assured me that this crust could survive even my "delicate" touch. The use of egg instead of water to bind the dough gives it a pale yellow cast and a lighter texture. — *Donna Kerr*

MAKES ONE 10-INCH CRUST

2 cups unbleached white flour

⅓ cup superfine sugar

Pinch of salt

1 egg

¾ cup (1½ sticks) sweet butter, cut in small pieces, at room
temperature

1 egg, beaten

1. Sift the flour, sugar, and salt in a mixing bowl. Make a well in the
center.
2. Add the whole egg. Begin blending with a mixer or pastry blender.
Add the butter gradually and continue blending until the butter almost
disappears. This should not take more than 45 seconds. Knead the
dough 2 or 3 times, form into a ball, and wrap in waxed paper.
Refrigerate 2 to 3 hours.
3. Preheat the oven to 425°.
4. Roll out the dough to ⅛ inch thick and line a 10-inch pie or tart pan.
Trim the edges.
5. Cover the dough with a piece of aluminum foil and weight it with rice
or beans. For a fully baked crust, bake about 20 minutes. Remove the
foil and weights and brush crust with some of the beaten egg. Continue
baking until the entire crust is lightly browned, about 5 minutes longer.
For a partially baked shell, bake with the foil and weights about 8
minutes. Remove the foil and weights, brush with beaten egg, and
return to the oven for another 4 minutes.

BASIC CRÊPES

I have fond memories of wandering around a country fair in Bordeaux,
France, savoring tasty crêpe suzettes. That was my first experience with the
versatile crêpe. Since then I have used this basic recipe many times. It is simple
and the variations are limitless, be it dessert or the main course. — *Tony Clark*

MAKES ABOUT 16 CRÊPES

1 cup unbleached white flour

Pinch of salt

4 eggs

¾ cup milk at room temperature

2 tablespoons sweet butter, melted

Sweet butter or oil for frying the crêpes

1. In a large bowl, mix together the flour and salt. Make a well in the center and put into it the eggs and 1 tablespoon of the milk. Beat them lightly with a fork or whisk. When combined, incorporate the egg mixture into the surrounding flour, whisking until the batter is smooth.

2. Gradually whisk in the milk and finally add the melted butter. Allow the mixture to rest one hour.

3. Heat a 6-inch crêpe pan with a little oil or butter over medium-high heat. When hot (being careful not to let the butter burn), pour in a large spoonful—about 2 to 3 tablespoons—of the batter and immediately tilt the pan so that the batter covers the entire surface. Remember, the thinner the better! Cook the crêpe until the bottom turns light brown, then flip and cook briefly on the other side.

4. Continue cooking crêpes in this manner, adding more butter or oil only as necessary. I find a pastry brush dipped in the oil or melted butter works well.

5. Stack the cooked crêpes, allow them to cool completely, then wrap tightly in plastic wrap and refrigerate or freeze until you're ready to use them. Allow crêpes to return to room temperature before filling them.

❦

SNIFF BISCUITS

Megan Sutton, manager of the ski shop, was the benefactor of this recipe. Sniff, everyone's favorite inn dog, was hopelessly addicted to the chocolate chip cookies. She especially enjoyed accompanying guests on the trail, as she knew they'd share with her the most coveted part of any trail lunch—the chocolate chip cookie. In order to break her of this habit (and help her maintain her girlish canine figure) I started baking these dog biscuits. This recipe, by the way, was requested almost as much as the recipe for chocolate chip cookies. — *Arlyn Hertz*

MAKES ABOUT 3 DOZEN SMALL DOG BISCUITS

> 1 cup unbleached white flour
> 1 cup whole wheat flour
> ½ cup wheat germ
> 1 tablespoon brown sugar
> 6 tablespoons salad oil
> 1 egg
> ½ cup milk
> 1 tablespoon or more cold water

1. Preheat the oven to 350°.
2. In a large bowl, mix together all of the dry ingredients. Beat in the oil, egg, milk, and water. Stir until well combined. If dough seems overly dry, add a little more water.
3. Roll out the dough to about ⅛ inch thick and cut out biscuits using animal-shaped cookie cutters.
4. Place biscuits on an ungreased cookie sheet and bake for about 15 minutes. Let the biscuits cool, then transfer them to an airtight container. Happy trails to you and your pet.

INDEX

INDEX

strawberry torte, 131
Millet, sunflower bread, 30
Mornay sauce, 93–94
Mousse: orange, 143–44
  salmon, 38
  strawberry, 144
Muffins: apple walnut, 22
  blueberry, 22–23
Mushrooms: with chicken breasts, 89–90
  sautéed shiitake with balsamic vinegar, 120
  stuffed, 46
  wild, 45–46
Mussels, steamed in white wine, 40
Mustard: cream sauce, 85–86, 97
  vinaigrette, 64–65

N
Nachos Christo, 53
Noodles, sesame, 51–52

O
Olive anchovy dip, 40
Omelet, French, 16
Orange: almond pancakes, 8
  cream icing, 26
  mousse, 143–44
Oranges Grand Marnier, 140–41

P
Pancakes: blueberry, 10
  orange almond, 8
  potato, 11–12
  puffed, 12
  raspberry, 9
Parfait, white velvet, 139
Papaya and avocado salad, 60–61
Pasta: with citrus beurre blanc, 50–51
  and shrimp, 42
Pâté: brisée, 156
  smoked fish, 38–39
Peach-blueberry pie, 133
Pears: champagne-poached, 141–42
  poached, 142
Peas, with fettucine, 49–50
Pepper: purée, 96–97
  salad, 62–63
Pesto sauce, 154
Pesto-stuffed chicken breasts, 93–94
Pie: latticed peach-blueberry, 133
  lime in meringue crust, 129
Pie crust, 155–56
  meringue, 129
  pâté brisée, 156
  sugar tart, 156–57
Pilaf, barley nut, 125
Pineapple with chocolate sauce, 139
Poached pears, 142
Poppy-seed cake, 128
Poppy seed salad dressing, 66

Pork: barbecued tenderloin, 84–85
  honey-smoked loin with mustard cream
    sauce, 85–86
  tenderloin medallions in vermouth-
    mustard sauce, 83–84
Potage: of minted snap peas and greens,
    69–70
  de Vermont, 76–77
Potato: in blueberry coffee cake, 25–26
  pancakes, 11–12
  and turnip purée, 119–20
Pudding, steamed raisin, 126
Puffed pancakes, 12
Purée: of lentil soup, 73–74
  potato and turnip, 119–20

Q
Quesadillas, 54
Quiche, crab, 39

R
Rainbow trout, with dilled hollandaise, 104
Raisin: pudding, 126
  sauce, 154–55
Raspberries, and ice cream, 143
Raspberry: crêpes, 136
  pancakes, 9
  vinaigrette, 62
Ravioli, lobster and crab, 112–14
Red-pepper coulis, 98–100
Rhubarb-strawberry crisp, 134
Rice: anti-restaurant, 123–24
  caraway and black olive, 124
  lentil and spices, 124
  tomato and basil, 124
  watercress and spice, 124
Roasted pepper salad, 62–63
Rolls, dill-caraway, 36

S
Salad dressings: Chèvre, 58
  green goddess herb, 65–66
  lemon-tarragon, 47–48
  poppy seed, 66
Salads: avocado and papaya, 60–61
  caesar, 58–59
  fennel, 59–60
  green, 58
  roasted pepper, 62–63
  spinach and goat cheese, 61
  summer bean, 62
Salmon: broiled topped with sauteed scallops,
    109–10
  in ginger-lime-sambuca sauce, 108
  mousse, 38
Salsa cruda, 153
Sauces: apple-pear, 11
  black currant, 12
  chocolate, 139